TOXIC PEOPLE-

They can be dangerous to your spirit!

Be Free In Jesus Name!

Prophetess Marshell Forte

Scripture quotations marked (NLT) are taken from the Holy Bible, New Living Translation, copyright © 1996, 2004, 2007 by Tyndale House Foundation. Used by permission of Tyndale House Publishers, Inc., Carol Stream, Illinois 60188. All rights reserved.

Scripture quotations marked (NIV) are taken from THE HOLY BIBLE, NEW INTERNATIONAL VERSION®, NIV® Copyright © 1973, 1978, 1984, 2011 by Biblica, Inc.® Used by permission. All rights reserved worldwide

Scriptures marked (NKJV) are taken from the New King James Version, © 1982 by Thomas Nelson, Inc. All rights reserved. Used by permission.

Copyright © 2013 Prophetess Marshell Forte

All rights reserved. No part of this publication may be reproduced, stored in a retrieval system, or transmitted in any form or by any means, electronic, mechanical, photocopying, recording, or otherwise, without the prior written permission of the publisher.

ISBN: 978-1-60383-473-5

Published by:
Holy Fire Publishing

www.ChristianPublish.com

Printed in the United States of America and the United Kingdom

~Dedicate This Book~

I dedicate this book to my Parents, my twin sister Michelle and my brother James. I Thank God for placing you all in my life and I love you more than you ever know! I know what God has for our family and it SHALL be restored in Jesus name! It's our destiny to succeed! It's in our blood line! Love you all---*Agape'*!

~Acknowledgments~

First of all, thank you Heavenly Father for giving me the courage to write this book. It took me awhile to comprehend what you were telling me Father but now I understand! I love you so much! I praise you El Shaddah!

To my loving husband, Jonathan "Jay" Forte; there aren't enough words to tell you how much I love you and thank you for your uncompromising support! Your prayers and your encouragements have helped me along the way. Especially, those times of my **"valley experience"** where I felt so alone! Thanks babe for not giving up on me when others have! God bless you and May God's divine favor continues to shine in and on you! Love you babe!

To my daughters: Janeka, Adrienne, DeAndrea "Dede" and Marlesha stay focus and never ever give up on your dreams!! Dream big, aim high and watch God move on your behalf! Love each other and support each other!! Most importantly pray for one another!! Momma loves you dearly-- my princesses'!

Special thanks to God parents: Mr. LeeDell Thornton (Dad), Mrs. Eleanor Thornton (Momma) and Ms. Kelli Thornton (God sister) for opening up your hearts to me. Words can't express the gratitude I feel right now. When I was in my lowest point in my life you all allow God to fill your hearts with so much love for me to accept me as your own! Even when I was rejected by my own you all still loved me unconditionally and never judge me! When I was disowned and told that I was a "NOBODY" you spoke life to me and said "I AM SOMEBODY!" Also when I was told I wouldn't amount to anything you spoke to my spirit man and said "I can do all things through Christ which strengthens me!" Thank you so much family I love you all so much and Daddy LeeDell if you are looking down on me I pray that I made you proud! (xoxo)

To Apostle Senordor M. SR and Prophetess Valencia D. Hines… again you two have been my rock in praying for me and my family! You are a "Diamond" that shines deeply in my heart! Thank you for answering the call in being my brother and sister! God knew there was a void in my life that needed to be filled!! I love you both and I speak divine favor over your lives and that you will continue to advance in the kingdom of God to the highest level! Nothing but "GREATNESS" Muah! Muah!

Big thanks to Marry Smith—(with two "Rs" SMILE) and Stephanie Watkins-Brown thank you for helping me during my time in need. I was in desperation and you saw me whom GOD had birthed in me. I thank you all for your sisterly love which was well received and needed! Love you much! To the rest of my family and friends (for there are too many to name) thank you, thank you, and I love you!!

~Interlude~

Get It Together My Sistah and My Brotha'

Get it together my sistah and my brotha',
This is only a trial that you are going through!

You have endured the best of the best,
In all your strength, press through this test!

Don't let the weight of this storm wear you down,
For Joy cometh in the morning, so don't wear a frown!

Press on and fight on, don't you dare give in,
For this I know, you shall surely win!

With this truth, God is protecting you from every hidden area,
Shielding you from the enemy's crooked barrier!

Hold on my sistah and my brotha just a little while longer,
For God is building you up and making you stronger!

Hold your head up high and be strong,
For Victory is on its way it won't be long!

You are Victorious, a Conqueror, and Mighty in Valor,
For God will never put anything on you that you can't handle!

Poem by
Prophetess Marshell D Forte

~Foreword~

The Apostle Paul made reference to Toxic Relationships in 1 Corinthians 15:33.

1 Corinthians 15:33 (AMP) **Do not be so deceived and misled! Evil companionships (communion, associations) corrupt and deprave good manners and morals and character.**

Although one may be a morally good person, you can have people in your life that can become toxic. In this revelatory book, "Toxic People – They Can Be Dangerous to Your Spirit" Prophetess Marshell Forte, has detailed a pattern on how to deal with people and situations that may detrimental to your personal and spiritual growth.

Beginning with "Toxic People-How Do You Recognize Them"? Prophetess Forte, illustrates how to recognize Toxic People and save yourself a lot of misfortune. By trusting the Word of God more than your emotions you can go from being in a state of despair to re-establishing yourself and having victory in every area of your life.

Hence, "Toxic People- They can Be Dangerous To Your Spirit", is a must read for anyone who may be in or has gone through a relationship that takes more than it gives or tears down rather than build up.

Apostle Senordor M. SR & Prophetess Valencia D. Hines
New Life House of Prayer Ministries International
www.nlhop.org

~Foreword~

"Have you been contaminated"? If so, Prophetess Marshell Forte' eloquently maps out the path to deliverance in this compelling book. Toxic People - They can be dangerous to your spirit: is filled with faith from cover to cover. Those that read this book will see extraordinary miracles in their lives when they take up the challenges this book offers. Prophetess Marshell writes in a way that will inspire, equip, and most importantly, invoke spiritual deliverance from strongholds. Once you recognize the toxic people in your life, chapter two (2) outlines how to 'break the cycle'. Chapter five (5) encourages us that through the power of God, and the blood of Jesus, we are winners.

If the Son therefore shall make you free, ye shall be free indeed. (John 8:36)

Pastor Jonathan Forte'
Overseer of Effective Ministries Family Worship Center, Inc.

nothing to hold me up. Listen, if you are not careful toxic people can make you feel and do some crazy things!

But GOD!! Thank God for freedom in Jesus-- I am no longer bound and under bondage *(Under captivity, servitude or compulsion)*! Galatians 5:1 NKJV states, ***"Stand fast therefore in the liberty by which Christ has made us free, and do not be entangled again with a yoke of bondage."*** Hallelujah! Like the commercial said, "I should have had a V8!" When God showed me of myself and who I am in Him and from the prayers of family/friends it was a wakeup call. So to say in reading this book, I pray that you will be free from Toxic people and also pled that you pray especially for those who have hurt you.

Listen beloved, WE ARE FREE and able to do what was impossible before-to live unselfishly! Jesus has freed us from the consequences of sin, from self-deception, and from deception by Satan and **Toxic People!!** As we seek to serve God, Jesus' perfect truth frees us to be all that God predestined us to be in Jesus Name. Amen!

Table of Contents

CHAPTER ONE
~Toxic People ~ How Do You Recognize Them?~ 17

CHAPTER TWO
~Break the Cycle~..31

CHAPTER THREE
~Protect Your Self Esteem~
Take Your Power Back!..79

CHAPTER FOUR
~Detach-Let Them Go!~..141

CHAPTER FIVE
~You Are A Winner!~..149

~Conclusion~...153

Endnotes:...161

CHAPTER ONE

~Toxic People ~ How Do You Recognize Them?~

Toxic people can be dangerous to your spirit! Only if you allow them to but you have to recognize and get rid of it! A toxic person can cause injury by his or her words. In Proverbs 18:21 KJV states, *"Death and life are in the power of the tongue: and they that love it shall eat the fruit thereof."* Also in Proverbs 13:3 NKJV states, *"He who guards his mouth preserves his life, but he who opens wide his lips shall have destruction."* When you allow the toxic venom of what others speak out and to seep in; it affects and contaminates everything in and around you!! To give a better analogy of what toxic is…*it's like cancer where it eats away your flesh but to end it before it goes through your entire body just like a cancer patient in order to fight this disease they must go through radiation/chemo to KILL IT!* Stop it before it spreads--does that makes sense??!

Self-control is not mastered if you do not control what you say. Words can cut and destroy. In James 3:5 NKJV states, *"Even so the tongue is a little member and boasts great things…."* If you want to be self-controlled, begin with your tongue. Stop and think before you react or speak toxicity. Examples of an untamed toxic tongue includes *gossiping, putting others down, bragging, manipulating, false teaching, exaggerating, complaining, flattering and lying.* If you can control this small but powerful member, you can control the rest of your body.

When looking up the word Toxic in the [4]Merriam-Webster online dictionary it means, "[1]*Containing or being poisonous material especially when capable of causing death or serious debilitation.* [2]*Exhibiting symptoms of infection or toxicosis <the patient became* toxic *two days later.* [3]*Extremely harsh, malicious, or harmful.* [4]*Containing or contaminated with a substance capable of injuring or killing a living thing <certain plants are* toxic *if eaten>*"

The word Toxic describes it well in the Thesaurus: *envenomed, poison, poisoned, toxic, venomous.* Here are more related words to toxic: *contagious, infectious, infective, pathogenic, pestilent, pestilential; baneful, deleterious, harmful, hurtful, injurious, malignant, nocuous, noxious, virulent; virulent; unhealthful, unhealthy, unwholesome; calamitous, deadly, fatal, lethal, murderous* and the list goes on and on!! There are many signs of recognizing toxic people in your life. This person may be spreading their negativity like a poison. So ask yourself this question right now!!! How many toxic people are spoiling your life right now? One? ...Two?...More?....Have you thinking huh…hmm right?!

Sometimes you may not be aware that person is being toxic until it catches you by surprise! You sense your attitude starts to change to negative or you're always in a bad mood. For instance, every time you come in contact of that toxic person it seems like a dark cloud succumbs you. At first you were in a "GREAT" mood and when that toxic person begins to talk it feels like all your energy has been drained out. Like a vacuum cleaner suctioning the very life out of you or a parasite sucking all the blood out of your veins. Leaving you feeling lifeless and despondent. So what do you do about it?????

Now there are those who may be aware what they are doing and intentionally want to be hurtful because of revenge or jealousy!! That is intimidating, manipulating and not godly!! Hosea 10:13 NIV, *"But you have planted wickedness, you have reaped evil, you have eaten the fruit of deception because you have depended on your own strength and on your many warriors."* People who fall for this type of toxic behavior are also capable of toxic manipulation, intimidation and lies of those who want to lead others astray. It's like a spider web--everywhere you turn you're caught in the strands of cobwebs.

Many of these people who are under the influence of that spirit of being Toxic have been endorsed by the devil to place venom in. I too have experienced toxic people in my life and not even realizing that venom seeping into my spirit! Especially in my younger years I have had a lot of exposure of toxicity going in and out of my life like a revolving door. Often times I would allow people to tell me who they thought I was in their own eyes because they didn't want me to advance and with their negative words they continue to pull me down! I wasn't strong enough to push them away or had the courage to use the WORD of God against the devices. I became crippled in their web of lies where I couldn't stand up for myself or recognize the winner that was inside of me! As children you are vulnerable and very fragile so words can hurt! You can't defend yourself! Tears flow, brick wall forms and all you see is yourself being the way people say you are!
In 1 Corinthians 3:15 states, *"Don't you know that you yourselves are God's temple and that God's Spirit lives in you?"*

For all those years not standing up or guarding myself I allowed those toxic words to lie dormant in my spirit for years-- not moving forward!! I became a doormat to others to walk on and a trash can to be dumped at any time! During those trying times, I didn't have any godly example on how to recognize those types of people or behavior! I didn't know the power of prayer to combat those weapons! I always battled by taking that same venom they gave me and passed it back to that person or onto another person that may not have caused the problem!! I felt I just needed to release it because of the built in frustration for years of being the victim! In 2 Corinthians 10:4 NLT states, *"We use God's mighty weapons, not worldly weapons, to knock down the strongholds of human reasoning and to destroy false arguments."*

Listen my beloved; please don't try to fix the problem or the person on your own! **Seek help!!** Whether; you are the problem or the other person who is toxic. When you chose to ignore it or dismiss it without getting help or refuge from someone like a minister or counselor it will become worse or better yet fatal to your spiritual growth/life or to others!! Psalm 37:39KJV states, *"But the salvation of the righteous is of the LORD: he is their strength in the time of trouble."* God is the source of all fixes in your lives. He will give you strength and the resource to seek help in the time of trouble.

Remember early in the chapter I told you that I didn't know how to handle toxic people better yet didn't have any help from a godly person… well for that voidance in my life I thought I had it all together. I left home at 18, joined the military (had to grow up fast but still not grounded or **GROWN!!**) and I ended up getting married at young age. But during those early years I didn't know anything about being married. I grew up in a home where affection wasn't shown a lot and also at times it was dysfunctional! Of course when it was special occasions (at times) **"it felt performed"** to love one another and especially in front of company but negativity still existed in the home! Now don't get me wrong every home is not perfect and there are shortcomings!! If anyone says that their home was like the "Cosby show or Brady bunch" then I believe that person may be lying (in my opinion) but if so then good for them but that would be unrealistic! There are some dysfunctional people out there especially when God isn't in the home for that you will certainly experience chaos and confusion!

In my parents' home, everyone on the outside looking in thought we were the perfect family! No one knew the hidden secrets that lay in our hearts of the abuse and verbal persecution that streamed out of the home. Please know that there is no perfect family! If there is no communication, no love, or godly example then it's not going to last or stand!! Mark 3:25 KJV states, *"And if a house be divided against itself, that house cannot stand!"*

We were all broken—from the head of the household all the way to the youngest child—EVERYONE!

In the point of my life when I just couldn't get it right as a teenager I ran away from home all the time; I ran from my problems and seeking someone to love me--for me no! Searching but no one was around or to be found!! From the verbal abuse in my parents' home where I was told that I was ugly, never amount to nothing, never make it in life, and will always be a failure! Those toxic venoms was deposited in my life and was rooted deep daily!! I felt so helpless and lost! To the point where I couldn't breathe or think for myself! I kept those negative thoughts which was toxic in my mind, my heart and believed every word of it! I did things that wasn't good as a child to gain some type of affection from my parents but it was at no avail. I needed someone to tell me that I was beautiful, loved and needed! Yes as a child I wasn't the brightest or perfect child (I hope you can attest that you did things that weren't pleasing to your parents and often time embarrassing) but again NO parents should disown/discredit their child!!

There were toxic signs visible in the home and often times we were too afraid to say or to speak out because of the fear that was inputted in our hearts. Control was evident and yet there was discipline but it was more in my opinion manipulation. Again, I am not saying I was a perfect child—I WASN'T!

With that said, if there is abusive in the home no child should become victims to that type of behavior regardless how **bad** (**b**lessed **a**nointed and **d**elivered) or misbehaved they are!! **NO** child should be a punching bag or words of hatred from their parents!! They are a gift from God! Psalm 127:3 NASB ***"Behold, children are a gift of the LORD; the fruit of the womb is a reward."*** Listen parents you have to be careful not to seep venom in your child (ren) lives because it will either reproduce to something negative and/or destructive behaviors! Yes children at times would need discipline. In Proverbs 13:24 NIV states, *"Whoever spares the rod hates their children, but the one who loves their children is careful to discipline them."* Now don't get a twisted the scripture doesn't say beat them till they bleed white/red or punch them where they face disfigured. That is not godly and not right!! Now, I have experienced and seen many children become defiant toward other people because of what was done to them and deposited in them by their loved ones! God is holding us accountable how we teach, train and live in front of our children! Proverbs 22:6KJV states, *"Train up a child in the way he should go: and when he is old, he will not depart from it."* Just because you are bigger you have no right to hurt NO ONE! YOU ARE TOXIC!! Ephesians 6:4 states, *"And, ye fathers, (and mothers) provoke not your children to wrath: but bring them up in the nurture and admonition of the Lord."* I truly believe this scripture should be applied as well…. to Aunts, Uncles, Grandparents, Siblings, boyfriends and girlfriends, babysitters, etc etc…..especially when the children are in their care! Yes you're accountable!!!

As you can see, I am very passionate in this area when it comes to being toxic towards children because what I have experienced. The only attention I received growing up was abusive words and fist! Now, I wasn't a perfect child and the things that I did to my parents…. well I deserved the punishment but many of the abuse I experienced I DID NOT! Listen all, I am not here to bad mouth my parents or make you all feel sorry for me; that's not my intention at all! What I am trying to do is expose the devil's ugly head and his tactics when it comes to toxic and sin!! For us as parents have to be careful when we are disciplining our children! I quote this scripture again….Proverbs 13:24 NIV *"Whoever spares the rod hates their children, but the one who loves their children is careful to discipline them."* Now don't get confused what it says…I did not say **hate** in word of toxic! This interpretation simply means do not withhold discipline from a child; if you punish him with the rod, he will not die. Never use violence to discipline your child(ren) but spank them when necessary and talk to them in LOVE on why they are being disciplined—never talk or spank them while you are heated or angry with them why you ask?? Because that is when words comes out and you end up abusing and then saying something you didn't want to say! Next thing you know retaliation from your child festers in their hearts and carries to their adulthood—hey I know because it happened to me!!

To get back to the subject at hand, during my parents' life growing up for them wasn't easy!! They didn't have a lot and the way the world is now of technology and computer age my parents didn't have that luxury! It was black and white TV or no TV at all. Hand me down clothes passed down from the oldest to younger siblings and grandma trying to make ends meet to feed her children where back in the day blacks was limited to the job market especially if you were a female! To top it off my grandpa died at an early age so that left my grandma raising all the children by herself. So imagine growing up in a household with a lot of people trying to gain attention from one person?! That must have been hard to do! Grandma was busy raising 13 to 15 children in the home or out working etc, etc! That left the children who were older thinking that grandma was showing favoritism/partiality to younger siblings or vice versa and that caused jealousy in the home between siblings. So when disagreements between the siblings occur they would hold grudges, toxic words are verbally expressed but all in all…. they all wanted love and attention from their Mother (which grandma to me). But how many can say that still happens with only 2 to 3 children in the home. So, in turn unforgiveness and bitterness settled in. For years not forgiving one another, holding grudges, not talking to one another, or not checking and loving on each other led to some of the family members disassociating with the family! The seed was planted and brewing!! So without realizing their parents (my grandparents) detached themselves from their children, causing division and discord, jealousy among themselves by not forgiving and for that a generational curse cycle continued downward to my parents, to their siblings then to my siblings. That is Toxic!! When some of the siblings tried to reach out to the ones who was disassociated it was misconstrued as playing favorites. See how the devil sneaks his ugly head in!!! When there is slight inclination of discord he comes in and cause riff raft amongst the family! Proverbs 22:10KJV, *"Cast out the scoffer, and contention shall go out; yea, strife and reproach shall cease."*

So we can see a person who is toxic causes discord through strife and divisions has a spiritual problem. Such a person is a scorner, a talebearer, angry, proud, forward, wrathful, wicked, and hateful spirited. This person is not happy if people are getting along. He/she is constantly causing people to fight with one another. That is a sign of being toxic!

This goes on in all walks of life. You see it in community gatherings, churches, businesses, schools. There are some people who have a spirit of divisiveness that drives them to bring toxic to people. Perhaps you have seen people like this. They are not happy when everything is running smoothly. If these people have a hidden agenda, they are bad news to the social order.

Have you ever experience this before? You are at work and as soon as this certain individual walk in the door/office you feel yourself sinking in the chair or hiding in another room. Well that may be a sign of that person has a toxic behavior. If you witnessed every single time that person opens their mouth it's always talking negative or always cursing to a point where it makes you gage then you have encountered a Toxic person! For me, there was a situation where this person always has to make a point about their favorite sport team and discredit others who try to challenge them. Yes I love football and basketball but when this individual comes in the room I cringe because out of their mouth is nothing but cursing and put downs. So what I do… I don't talk about sports with that individual or better yet I change my surrounding.

Okay another situation, someone who appears to be nice to you in public but as soon as you turn your back they are constantly talking bad about you to others. I know you are not supposed to care what others say about you or to you but when they are being "fake-nice" then that is where I have a problem……that is toxic! I tend to stay away from people like that.. at least asks God to give me discernment how to handle those type of people because truth to be told its hard to love them in my flesh! So in turn I realize I must continue to love them despite how they treat me…In Luke 6:28(NIV) states, **"Bless those who curse you, pray for those who mistreat you!"**

Most of us can come up with a mile-long list of people who've made us miserable, some time or the other - teachers, classmates, brothers, sisters, parents, friends, colleagues… while you were allowing them to make you feel angry, confused and irritated, unknown to you, they were seriously damaging your health. In other words, they were toxic. But we have a remedy for this type of behavior!! In Hebrews 2:8 NKJV states, **"You have put all things in subjection under his feet. For in that He put all in subjection under Him.** Now when it says "all things," it means nothing is left out. But we have not yet seen all things put under their authority. In other words, when you are confused by the present events and anxious about the future and what others have done to hurt you…remember that Jesus true position and authority. He is Lord of all not your present circumstances!! One day He will rule on earth as He does now in heaven. He will step in your situation, take them away and put those circumstances under your feet!! Halleluiah! Now that is something to shout about… don't you agree?!

Here's another example of someone being toxic: I received a 2 a.m. phone call, with a friend pouring her heart out about the latest disaster in her life. Love her as I do, 2 a.m. isn't my best time - especially when I've got an early start and a body that needs at least eight hours of uninterrupted sleep.

Still, have you ever tried saying no to a friend in need? Exactly!!

So you end up spending an hour saying yes and no in all the right places, then get a headache and take refuge in a cup of coffee.

After listening to your dear friend pour her heart to you, probing the answers to correct the wrong that may or may not have happened, giving encouraging words and being sympathetic to cause at hand. You suddenly feel drained, not because your desire is to help but it seems like the same person keeps calling you at the exact time- every single day and finding that you have already given them the godly advice the day before to them?! And nothing in their life has changed for the better but they want to get the sound advice from you! All of sudden you see a "caution light flashing fiercely" WARNING! WARNING!! "Anyone who manages to drag you down, make you feel angry, worn out, deflated, belittled or confused…." <u>IT'S A SIGN OF A TOXIC PERSON!</u>

Most of us can come up with a list, as long as our arm, of people who've made us feel miserable - starting with teachers and bullies at school, moving on to brothers, sisters, boyfriends, bosses and so-called friends. Not forgetting arrogant doctors and road hogs.

But what makes a toxic person tick? "They're people whose feelings of insecurity and inadequacy make them jealous, envious and uncaring, so they end up sabotaging your projects, your relationships, your happiness-even your car journey!" (Driving in Kuwait with the non driving people who got their license from Cracker Jack box…can make you angry). It could be the temperamental boss who's never satisfied, the friend who knows where you're going wrong (and revels in telling you), or the critical parent who can't stop treating you like a BAD ten-year-old.

But whatever your own personal definition of a toxic person, one thing is certain - putting up with a toxic relationship can seriously damage your health. "Migraines, eye-twitches, skin rashes and eating disorders often have their roots in toxic relationship that have gone on for too long."

Listing the people and types of behavior that get to you is the first step to detoxing your relationships - and your life. (And, believe it or not, that's the easy bit!) But the good news is there are ways of responding that can stop you being the victim of toxic behavior. 1 Peter 4:12 NIV, *"Dear friends, do not be surprised at the painful trial you are suffering, as though something strange were happening to you"*

I can recall a time where I was having a "pity party" moment crying and sad all day! My husband asked me what was wrong and I told him *"Why my parents rejected me? Why I can't be close to my siblings? And why can't I have a family closeness like you have with your family?"* And you know what!! My husband looked at me and without blinking said *"who are you and what does the word say?"* Now who wants to hear that?? I was at my **"pity party"** moment and I didn't want to hear that but the Jesus in my husband knew it was needed!! My husband knew what would shake me into reality and back to my sanity!! He quoted Jeremiah 1:5 NKJV *"**Before I formed you in the womb I knew you; before you were born I sanctified you; I ordained you a prophet to the nations!**"* God knew what I would be going through before I was ever formed!! He knew the trials and tribulations I will encounter. He knew I will be rejected, lied on; not loved; scorned; betrayed; misunderstood; dismissed; etc etc….for that he ordained me and prepared me to be a prophet to the nations!! You asked why?? Well…Why not?? Jesus went through it so why am I so different?!

Also my husband quoted another scripture that just messed me up-- SERIOUSLY!! In Psalms 27:10 NKJV states, *"When my father and my mother forsake me, then the Lord will take care of me!"* In other words you may have had the sad experience of being forsaken by father or mother. Or even both!! Broken homes, difference of beliefs, addiction to drugs or alcohol, even psychological isolation can leave you crippled by the loss. As adults the pain may linger but God can take that place in our life, fill that void, and heal that hurt. He can direct us to people who may take the role of father, mother, brother or sister for us. His love is sufficient for all our needs! For that I truly thank God for the spiritual mothers and spiritual siblings in my life!! Halleluiah! We serve an awesome God who meets our every need!! Jehovah Jireh!

CHAPTER TWO

~Break the Cycle~

Here are some more examples of toxic relationships. Fathers who are only interested in their sons if they "measure up" as far as career and athletics go or Sisters, who compete with one another to the point of betrayal or Mothers, who are overly critical of their daughters. Drama seeking in laws as well as busy body's looking for something to gossip about at the expense of others all fit the bill as far as toxic relationships are concerned. Proverbs 26:17 KJV states, *"He that passes by, and meddles with strife belonging not to him, is like one that takes a dog by the ears."* In other words taking a dog by the ears is a good way to get bitten, and interfering in arguments is a good way to get hurt. It is best simply to keep out of arguments that are none of your business.

These relationships affect not only one's self esteem but general sanity at times. These types of relationships are never healthy. There is a school of thought that one's emotions can affect one's overall health. If you are emotionally disturbed you likely will manifest those feeling into **"dis-ease"** or another physical ailment. When your emotions start to affect you physically it is time to do something about the toxic people in your life. BREAK THE CYCLE! Jesus warns about this for it brings division!! In Luke 12:52-53 NKJV states, *"For from now on five in one house will be divided: three against two, and two against three. Father will be divided against* *son and son against Father, mother against daughter and daughter against mother, mother-in-law against her daughter-in-law and daughter-in-law against mother-in-law."*

This is evident today of above scripture. I just read the other day a famous football player got into an altercation with his mom and decided to become physical abusive with her in public. With no regards just became irate, violent and disrespectful towards his mother which landed him in jail and a FAT fine! Jealousy amongst siblings because one is not where they should be so in turn they want to bring havoc in the family instead of helping one another. This toxic behavior! (Spirit of bigotry and persecution that will break through the strongest bonds of relationship and natural affection.

Another incident: where a mother decided that she didn't want to be a parent and decided to drown all three of her children in the bathtub. One by one she drowned her helpless babies but before doing that complained and cried help for months to her husband that she didn't feel right in her body and needed help but was told, *"You will be fine it's just post-partum depression."* See the signs!! Here is another incident of a Father decided to shoot his wife because he didn't want to pay child support! The list goes on and on…toxic is becoming the norm. God forbid!

Remember earlier when I was talking about **Toxic** becoming venom. Let's reverse this, say that you are the one who is toxic. Well when you don't realize the importance of this it can become dangerous in your spiritual walk and/or your everyday life. You become oblivious and blind to what is around you that you contaminate everyone you come in contact with! You wonder why your marriage is on shaken ground because of the negativity energy you bring into it and around you. You wonder why your co-workers can't get along with you! You wonder why you are always sad, lonely, depressed, angry, bitter and not happy. Envying other people lifestyle and jealous to the point of complaining of not having enough. Blaming others for your mishaps or shortcomings in life! In James 3:14 KJV states, **"But if you harbor bitter envy and selfish ambition in your hearts, do not boast about it or deny the truth."** In other words: bitterness, envy and self-seeking are inspired by the devil. It is easy to be drawn into wrong desires by the pressures of society and sometimes by well-meaning toxic people who claim they are Christians. By listening to the advice, "Assert yourself," Go for it," "Set high goals," we can be drawn into greed and destructive competitiveness. Instead we must seek God's wisdom which will deliver us from the need to compare ourselves to others and to want what they have!

Many people are in **relationships** that are unhealthy. However, when a person is in the middle of this relationship, it is often difficult to see how detrimental the relationship is to his or her self-esteem. Others may tell you that your partner is "no good for you" or "that they can't understand why you don't leave when you are being abused?!" Your spouse may be a good provider, a good father, a good mother and at times, loving and kind to you. However, there are other times when you are left feeling alone, afraid, or upset and don't understand what is going on. A great analogy of a toxic person is *"anyone who manages to drag you down, make you feel angry, worn out, deflated, belittled or confused."* It may be difficult for people to admit they are in a toxic relationship, because they are intelligent, self-sufficient individuals in other aspects of their lives. Most people in toxic relationships, however, have the sense that something is just not right.

I remember I was in a relationship before I met my husband Jay. I was involved with this man who I thought was for me. I recently divorced from a broken marriage but was emotionally involved with someone who knew I was vulnerable. I didn't allow God to heal me from hardship, pain, anguish, unforgiveness and bitterness!

After being married for 14yrs and then divorced I thought "this man" would take away all the hurt and the pain I was feeling but all in all that wasn't the case. He kept telling me that he loved me and cared for me but his actions were totally different. After two years of going back and forth with this "guy" lying and cheating I had enough of battling with someone who was using me, controlling, abusive and manipulating me! I had to take a step back and ask myself.. *"Why in the world would I allow this cycle to take place again after going through almost a similar experience in my marriage prior?"* During the two years of dating him I always made excuses for his actions toward me and compromising my integrity to be with him who didn't love me back! Why? Yes, yes I know I wasn't thinking!! But you know what I did…. I finally let that joker go! Like that song from [10]R Kelly "When a Woman's Fed up!" Yeah! Lesson learned and eyes wide opened! Thank you JESUS!

I wonder if you heard any of your family members or friends say this.... "*I love God and he knows my heart* and *if they don't want to talk to me then, so be it... I will cut them off!!* Or "*I can't stand them anyway so why should I try to help then!!*" Or "*my hands are completely washed from them all together.*" Or "*I won't have anything to do with them even if they are related to me or not!!*" But, God words says that **"If someone says, I love God, and hates his brother, he is a liar; for he who does not love his brother whom he has seen, how can he love God whom he has not seen? And this commandment we have from Him: the he who loves God must love his brother also." 1 John 4:20-21 NKJV.** In other words, it's easy to say we love God when that love doesn't cost us anything more than weekly attendance at a church service. But the real test of our love for God is how we treat the people right in front of us-our family members, friends and fellow believers. Also those we call "associates." We cannot truly love God while neglecting to love those who are created in His image. God's love is the source of all human love, and it spreads like fire. In loving his children, God kindles a flame in their hearts. In turn, they love others, who are warmed by God's love through them. Another scripture that comes to mind is John 13:34 NKJV states, "*A new commandment I give to you, that you love one another; as I have loved you, that you also loved one another.*" We are to love others based on Jesus sacrificial love for us. Such love will not only bring unbelievers and Toxic people to Christ; it will also keep them strong and united in a world hostile to God.

Here are more signs on how to recognize toxic people: Have you noticed on your job or at school that there is that certain individual who tends to dump their anger or frustration to you as though you are their **"Personal garbage can!"** They nag and complain all the time! Everything is not right in their eyes! When you go to try to calm him or her down all they would do is rant and rave about everything that is wrong in their life or their job situation. Then the next thing happens, you'd grow more and more unhappy listening to them until they went back to whatever they were doing leaving you feeling bad for some time. In Philippians 2:14 NKJV states, ***"Do all things without complaining and disputing."*** Now if all that you do is complain, constantly argue and gossip you are sending a false impression of Christ and the gospel. There is a big difference between venting and finding resolution versus someone complaining and becoming toxic in their speech with no solution to their problem…does that make sense?! Our lives should be characterized by moral purity, patience and peacefulness, so that we will "shine as lights" in a dark and toxic depraved world. A transformed life is an effective witness to the power of God's Word. In Philippians 2:15 NKJV states, ***"that you will become blameless and harmless, children of God without fault in the midst of a crooked and perverse generation, among whom you shine as lights in the world, holding fast the word of life, so that I may rejoice in the day of Christ that I have not run in vain or labored in vain."***

Have you ever had that happen to you? Well I did! I felt drained and overwhelmed! I had a co-worker do that to me.

Eventually, I noticed that after she unloaded her anger onto me, she was cheerful. She had successfully transferred all the negative energy to me and could continue her day in a better frame of mind. This was the first time I recognized toxicity in another person. This woman wasn't entirely toxic. She could be gracious and helpful, and in fact, when I had surgery on my hand back in 2002 (carpal tunnel syndrome) she was the only one of my co-workers to offer assistance by carrying my bags and helping with my paperwork chores. Once I knew not to absorb her negativity, we had few problems working together. For that, I'd begun to learn a valuable lesson: **there are toxic people in the world.**

A toxic person drains your energy. It may be that they get you to spend a lot of time and emotional strength trying to cheer them up. They may bombard you with their negativity so that you have to spend energy trying to fend it off. Perhaps their constant pessimism infects you, or they always make you angry. They may become leeches who feed themselves by making you give them your positivity. Its okay to help some people but don't allow anyone to be a dumping ground for them! In Jude 16 states, *"These are grumblers, complainers, walking according to their own lusts; and they mouth great swelling words, flattering people to gain advantage."*

Grumblers: "These men Jude is saying are complaining against God and his directions for living, preferring their own way-but then blaming God for anything that goes wrong for them."[1]

"They follow their own evil desires, for they reject divine authority.' To them self-discipline and self-control are nothing; to them the moral law is only a burden and a nuisance; honor and duty have no claim upon them; they have no desire to serve and no sense of responsibility.'"[2]

Loud Boasters: They boast of themselves because they have no confidence that their teachings are of God and so they promote themselves to their shame.

Of grumblers and malcontents (fault finders): "Grumblers are people who mutter against others under their breath, whereas malcontents are those who are always looking for ways in which they can attack and disparage everything and everybody."[3]

Do you know someone who always makes you feel depressed, angry or just plain tired? Think about this person. Is he or she a complainer, or someone who always expects things to go wrong, or someone who constantly finds fault with you? Does he or she always seem more cheerful after ranting to you? If any one or more of these is the case, you likely have a toxic person on your hands. Listen you may have to let that person know if they have a problem with that person for them to go to that person and fix it! In Matthew 18:15 NIV states, *"If your brother sins against you, go and show him his fault, just between the two of you. If he listens to you, you have won your brother over."* Also if you are the person who is having the problem with that individual--don't complain about it or be a toxic dumpster to someone else but go and get it right! When someone wrongs us, we often do the opposite of what Jesus recommends. We turn away in hatred or resentment, seek revenge, or engage in gossip! By contrast, we should go to that person first, as difficult as that may be.

Then we should forgive that person as often as he or she needs it. This will create a much better chance of restoring the relationship instead of it being a toxic relationship.

Now if you have tried all of this and that person is still toxic it's time to let them go. As the cliché says, "shake the dust off and move on!" Well in Matthew 10:14 NKJV states, ***"And whoever will not receive you nor hear your words, when you depart from that house or city, shake off the dust the dust from your feet."*** This action will show that you are not responsible for how people respond to you when you are rejected by toxic people. But, if you have an easy way to get this person entirely out of your life, you'll be better off instantly. Of course, often it is not so easy, when the toxic person is a co-worker or family member or even a long-time friend. If it's a co-worker, is there a good excuse like (not lying okay) "I'm right under an air vent that's chilling me" to get your desk moved? I know that may be a little dramatic but do you get the picture?? Perhaps you can say, *"You really ought to talk to the supervisor/manager about this"* and calmly return to doing your work.

With family members and friends, it may be more difficult. A seriously toxic friend may require that you gradually decrease the time you spend with this person over a period of months so it isn't particularly noticeable. When the toxic person is a family member, it may be possible to get the person into therapy, which is often needed to solve the underlying issue behind the negativity. If not, you need to train yourself to **"tune out"** when the complaining, fault-finding and energy-draining behavior starts.

Steps to Handle Toxic people

1. **Avoid toxic people**

I believe the best way to deal with toxic people is to not deal with them at all; to avoid them. In some cases it may not be an option, but more often than not, it is. This is why I encourage you to really think about the options you truly have with every toxic person in your life. It is common to think you have to deal with someone, when you actually do not. It is also common to believe you can get a toxic person to change while interacting with them. My experience is that unless you are a professional, you will not get them to change and trying it simply is not worth it. Go to prayer and ask God for wisdom to deal with them. In Jude 20-21 NKJV states, *"But you, beloved, building yourselves up on your most holy faith, praying in the Holy Spirit, keep yourself in the love of God, looking for the mercy of our Lord Jesus Christ unto eternal life."*

2. **Anticipate toxic people**

It is harder than usual to get out of relationships with a toxic person. Toxic people tend to have this ability to make you feel bad for avoiding them and to attach to you like a leech. This is why it's important to be able to spot them quickly, and start avoiding them before the relationship truly develops.

The best way I know to do this is to come up with a list of *clues* which you believe might indicate a toxic person. Then, every time you meet a person and a significant number of these *clues* are there, distance yourself from that person. Also what's helpful is asking God to give you discernment. In 1

Corinthians 2:14 NKJV states, *"But the natural man does not receive the things of the Spirit of God, for they are foolishness to him; nor can he know them, because they are spiritually discerned."*

3. Set firm boundaries

Toxic people will often use you, one way or another. They may complain to you all the time while you listen hopelessly (?), or they may constantly get you to get them out of trouble. This is where boundaries come in. *Boundaries are reflections of what you are and are not willing to do.*

Setting firm boundaries means not allowing toxic people to use you in any of these ways. It means refusing to listen to them complain, refusing to get them out of trouble. When you have firm boundaries, there is basically nothing bad any person can do to you. In Proverbs 22:24 ESV states, *"Make no friendship with a man given to anger, nor go with a wrathful man...."* Another good one is Philippians 4:8 ESV, *"Finally, brothers, whatever is true whatever is honorable, whatever is just, whatever is pure, whatever is lovely, whatever is commendable, if there is any excellence, if there is anything worthy of praise, think about these things."*

4. Get over your guilt

Most toxic people are very skilled at making others feel guilty when YOU don't do what they want. This makes it particularly hard to set and maintain firm boundaries with them. But, there is a way out of this dilemma: getting rid of your guilt. *It is your own guilt which toxic people use to break down your boundaries.*

When you can set and maintain boundaries with them without feeling guilty, the weapon they have against you is gone. Realize that your guilt is irrational, pointless, and it is used against you by toxic people. This is the best way to get over it. In Romans 3:19 NKJV states, *"Now we know that whatever the law says, it says to those who are under the law, that every mouth may be stopped, and all the world may become guilty before God"* In other words what I am saying is that when was the last time someone accused you of wrongdoing or making you feel guilty of something you did or didn't do? What was your reaction? Denial, argument and defensiveness? The bible tells us the world stands silent and accountable before Almighty God. (1 Corinthians 4:6 NIV states, *"Now, brothers and sisters, I have applied these things to myself and Apollos for your benefit, so that you may learn from us the meaning of the saying, "Do not go beyond what is written." Then you will not be puffed up in being a follower of one of us over against the other."*) No excuses or arguments are left. Have you reached the point with God where you are ready to hang up your defenses of being toxic and await his decision? If you haven't, stop now and admit your sin and get it right. I like how in[11]Matthew Henry Commentary talks about in scripture 1 Corinthians 4:1-6 about strife, take a look and read it for yourself… *"Apostles were no more than servants of Christ, but they were not to be undervalued. They had a great trust, and for that reason, had an honourable office. Paul had a just concern for his own reputation, but he knew that he who chiefly aimed to please men, would not prove himself a faithful servant of Christ. It is a comfort that men are not to be our final judges. And it is not judging well of ourselves, or justifying ourselves, that will prove us safe and happy. Our own judgment is not to be depended upon as to our faithfulness, any more than our own works for our justification.*

There is a day coming, that will bring men's secret sins into open day, and discover the secrets of their hearts. Then every slandered believer will be justified, and every faithful servant approved and rewarded. The word of God is the best rule by which to judge as to men. Pride commonly is at the bottom of quarrels. Self-conceit contributes to produce undue esteem of our teachers, as well as of ourselves. We shall not be puffed up for one against another, if we remember that all are instruments, employed by God, and endowed by him with various talents."

5. Do not defend yourself

When you avoid toxic people and you set boundaries with them, they frequently resort to accusing you, complaining and playing the victim in an attempt to get you to change your behavior.

One of the worst things you can do when this happens is to defend yourself. It is usually a futile action and it only keeps an immature dialog going which eventually helps the toxic person get what they want. You won't get anywhere with them by defending yourself and your actions.

Unfortunately, toxic people are everywhere. And they tend to attach themselves to those persons who are kind and have the most to offer. When you have the people skills to deal effectively with toxic people, you have the option to respond to their attaching in the best ways for you.

As for helping toxic people change their ways, I encourage you to leave/pass this task to the professionals in this area.

In Romans 8:1-2 NKJV states, *"There is therefore now no condemnation to those who are in Christ Jesus who do not walk according to the Spirit. For the law of the Spirit in Christ Jesus has made me free from the law of sin and death."* If you heard the words "Not guilty, let him go free"—what would those words mean to you if were on death row? The fact is that the whole human race is on death row, justly condemned for repeatedly breaking God's holy law. Without Jesus we would have no hope at all. But thank God! He has declared us not guilty and has offered us freedom from sin and power to do his will! We are no longer bound by toxic people! They no longer can make us feel guilty for not doing what they want us to do!!

Recognizing the signs of toxic love relationship

How do you tell if it's a toxic love relationship you are involved in? If it makes you sick - emotionally, mentally, and then physically, you are involved in toxic love with a person whom you are allowing to harm you. The love of God sustains, supports, gives, puts the other person first, puts the other person's interests above its own and is offered and given out of fullness, out of that life of God on the inside. In 1 John 4:7-8 NKJV states, *"Beloved, let us love one another, for love is of God; and everyone who loves is born of God and knows God. He who does not love does not know God, for God is love!"* Everyone believes that love is important, but love is usually thought of as a feeling. In reality, love is a choice and an action, as 1 Corinthians 13:4-7 shows, God is the source of our love; he loved us enough to sacrifice his Son for us, Jesus is our example of what it means to love; everything he did in life and death was supremely loving. (1 Corinthians 13:4-7 NIV states, *"Love is patient, love is kind. It does not envy, it does not boast, it is not proud. It does not dishonor others, it is not self-seeking, it is not easily angered, it keeps no record of wrongs. Love does not delight in evil but rejoices with the truth. It always protects, always trusts, always hopes, always perseveres."*)

Toxic love says, "Please, please love me. Please be to me what I need. Please fill this empty place in me." And that can never happen because nothing can ever fill that empty place except the love of God. No human being has what it takes to satisfy your hunger for love. God created that hunger for Himself.

God's love says, "I have so much, I am so full I want to share it with you. God is moving me to pour out some of His fullness out of myself into you." (Matthew 5:6, *"Blessed are those who hunger and thirst for righteousness, for they shall be filled"*)

One of the easiest ways in which people become involved in a toxic love relationship is with an addict or an alcoholic or with someone else who cannot have a healthy relationship because they are consumed by a need for what they are addicted to. To these people, while they can be deceitfully charming, other human beings are of little worth. They are to be used and when they lose their usefulness, they are expendable.

If you get into a relationship with one of these people, you are setting yourself up for heartache and hurt because they are totally consumed with themselves and what they want and need. Then they will draw you into their illness through toxic love.

Love shouldn't hurt, drag you through an emotional roller coaster or leave you feeling like less of a person. In 1 Corinthians 13:4 NKJV states, *"Love suffers long and is kind; love does not envy; love does not parade itself and is not puffed up!"* It can be very hard to realize when you're in a toxic relationship. You may ignore friends or family when they show concern or question the relationship. If you're reading this, something in you wants to know if this is describing you or someone you know. Then…Let's go deeper….. also in verse 5 in 1 Corinthians states, *"Love does not behave rudely, does not seek its own, is not provoked, and thinks no evil."* God's kind of love is directed outward toward others, not inward toward ourselves. It is utterly unselfish. This kind of love goes against our natural inclinations. It is possible to practice this love only if God helps us set aside our own desires and instincts, so that we can give love while expecting nothing in return. Thus the more we become like Christ, the more love we show to others.

Let's look at the multiple poisons a bad relationship can embody:

The abuser: you walk on eggshells trying to not say or do the wrong thing; after all he/she made it clear that their happiness is based on your actions. Abuse may be mental, physical or both. This abuse, I feel, is the most toxic because it whittles away at who you are. If they physically abuse you, they will repeat the offense.

Unrealistic Expectations: The abuser may expects you to be the perfect husband, wife, mother, father, lover, and friend. He/she is very dependent on you for all his/her needs, and may tell you he/she can fulfill all your needs as lover, friend, and companion. Statements such as: 'If you love me, I'm all you need.', 'You are all I need.' are common. Your abuser may expect you to provide everything for him/her emotionally, practically, financially or spiritually, and then blame you for not being perfect or living up to expectation.

The controller: he/she needs to know where you are at all times, you have no freedom. The same rule does not apply to them. You are to give them space and freedom, let them go when and where they please. This is toxic because you are always on edge, feeling like a teen that needs to check in with their parents.

You can't relax, ever, because they might call, text nor need you do something for them. Controlling behavior is often disguised or excused as concern. Concern for your safety, your emotional or mental health, the need to use your time well, or to make sensible decisions. Your abuser may be angry or upset if you are 'late' coming back from work, shopping, visiting friends, etc., even if you told him/her you would be later back than usual. Your abuser may question you closely about where you were, whom you spoke to, the content of every conversation you held, or why you did something he/she was not involved in. As this behavior gets worse, you may not be allowed to make personal decisions about the house, clothing, and going to church or how you spend your time or money or even make you ask for permission to leave the house or room. Alternately, he/she may theoretically allow you your own decisions, but penalize you for making the wrong ones. Concern for our loved ones to a certain extent is normal - trying to control their every move is not.

Starting sex while you are sleeping, demanding sex when you are ill or tired, or refusing any form of intimacy unless you are willing to go 'all the way' can all be signs that he/she could be sexually abusive or sexually violent.

Verbal Abuse: In addition to saying things that are meant to be cruel and hurtful, either in public or in private, this can include degrading remarks or running down any accomplishments. Often the abuser will tell you that you are 'stupid', could not manage without him/her. He/she may keep you up all night to 'sort this out once and for all' or even wake you at night to continue to verbally abuse you. The abuser may even say kindly things to your face, but speak badly about you to friends and family.

Dr. Jekyll and Mr. Hyde: (I would call this type bipolar.)Very rarely do abusers conform to the stereotypical image of a constantly harsh, nasty or violent person, either in public or in private. More frequently the abuser portrays a perfectly normal and pleasant picture to the outside world (often they have responsible jobs or are respected and important members of the local community or Church) and reserves the abuse for you in the privacy of your own home. Nor are abusers always overtly abusive or cruel, but can display apparent kindness and consideration. This Jekyll and Hyde tendency of the abuser serves to further confuse the victim, while protecting themselves from any form of suspicion from outsiders. Many victims describe "sudden" changes in mood - one minute nice and the next explosive or hysterical, or one minute happy and the next minute sad. This does not indicate some special "mental problem" but are typical of abusive personalities, and related to other characteristics such as hypersensitivity.

Drink or Substance Abuse: While neither drinking or the use of drugs are signs of an abusive personality, heavy drinking or drug abuse may be a warning sign and do increase the risks of abuse, especially violence, taking place. Often an abusive person will blame the drink for his/her abuse. However, a person who, knowing there is a risk he/she could be violent when drinking or on drugs, chooses to get drunk or high is in effect choosing to abuse. The link between substance abuse and domestic abuse is still being researched, and it is apparent that while neither alcohol nor drugs necessarily cause violence, they do increase the risk of violence.

History of Battering or Sexual Violence: Very rarely is abuse or violence a one-off event: a batterer will beat any woman he is with; a sexually abusive person will be abusive toward all his intimate partners. Situational circumstances do not make a person an abusive personality. Sometimes friends or family may try to warn you about the abuser. Sometimes the abuser may tell you himself/herself that he/she has hit or sexually assaulted someone in the past. However, they may further go on to explain that "she made me do it by ..." or in some other way not take responsibility and shift the blame on to the victim. They may tell you that it won't happen with you because "you love them enough to prevent it" or "you won't be stupid enough to wind me up that much". Once again, this is denying their own responsibility for the abuse, and shifting the responsibility for the relationship to remain abuse-free on to you. Past violence is one of the strongest pointers that abuse will occur. This is occurring a lot more than ever!!

Threatening Violence: This would obviously include any threat of physical force such as "If you speak to him/her again, I'll kill you", or "If any wife of mine acted like John's did, I'd give her a right seeing to". But can also include less obvious threats, such as "If you leave me, I will kill myself". Threats are designed to manipulate and control you, to keep you in your place and prevent you making your own decisions. Most people do not threaten their mates, but an abuser will excuse this behavior by saying "everybody talks like that.", maintaining he/she is only saying this because the relationship or you are so important to him/her, tell you you're "over-sensitive" for being upset by such threats, or obviously want to hurt him/her.

Breaking or Striking Objects: The abusive person may break your treasured object, beat his/her fists on the table or chair or throw something at or past you. Breaking your things is often used as a punishment for some imagined misdeed on your part. Sometimes it will be justified by saying that now that you are with him/her, you don't need these items any more. Breaking your possessions also has the effect of de-personalizing you, denying you your individuality or literally trying to break links to your past. Beating items of furniture or throwing objects will often be justified by saying you wound him/her up so much they lost control, once again shifting the blame for this behavior on to you, but is actually used to terrorize you into submission. Only very immature or abusive people beat on objects in the presence of other people in order to threaten or intimidate them.

Any Force during an Argument: An abuser may physically restrain you from leaving the room, lash out at you with his/her hand or another object, pin you against a wall or shout 'right in your face'. Basically any form of force used during an argument can be a sign that actual violence is a strong possibility.

Rigid Gender Roles: Abusers usually believe in stereotypical gender roles. A man may expect a woman to serve him; stay at home, obey him in all things - even things that are criminal in nature. A male abuser will often see women as inferior to men, more stupid, unable to be a whole person without a relationship. Female abusers may expect the man to provide for them entirely, shift the responsibility for her well-being onto him or heckle him as being 'not a real man' if he shows any weakness or emotion.

The manipulator: you are a puppet, they are the master, they know just which buttons to push, which strings to pull and your emotions become their game. Often they are selfish or self-centered people, concerned only with their needs and find ways to get the reaction or action out of you that they want. This can literally lead to your demise as they rob you of your own thoughts and steal your ability to feel good without them. This toxic form often leads to suicide, your desperation to escape.

Toxic relationships can be the hardest to end. If you live with them (*hope that you are not; especially married but that is another book*), it will take planning and support to safely leave and begin your life again without them, if possible stay with someone you trust during the transition. If you are not living together you must take steps to assure your safety and you must cut the ties completely. If you let them in your life, only a tiny bit, they will begin taking over again.

It will take all your inner strength to end a toxic relationship because they have stripped away so much of you and created fear, and hurt where they used to be joy. But you can do it, you can begin again. **1 Timothy 4:4 states,** *"For everything God created is good, and nothing is to be rejected if it is received with thanksgiving,")* Listen everything God created is good but this doesn't mean that we should abuse or be abused what God has made. Instead of abusing, we should enjoy the one God blessed us with which is a gift by serving and honoring them at the same time honoring God. Your life will begin once the toxic poison ends.

In contrast, the love of God says to these people, *"I will pray for you and I will give you the same choice God gives you - to make your own decisions and your own choices about your life and to suffer the consequences."* In Matthew 5:43-48 states, **"You have heard that it was said, 'Love your neighbor and hate your enemy.' But I tell you, love your enemies and pray for those who persecute you, that you may be children of your Father in heaven. He causes his sun to rise on the evil and the good, and sends rain on the righteous and the unrighteous. If you love those who love you, what reward will you get? Are not even the tax collectors doing that? And if you greet only your own people, what are you doing more than others? Do not even pagans do that? Be perfect, therefore, as your heavenly Father is perfect."** If you love your enemies and treat them well, you will truly show that Jesus is Lord of your life. This is possible only for those who give themselves fully to God, because only He can deliver people from natural selfishness and toxic behaviors.

(We can be perfect if our behavior is appropriate for our maturity level—perfect, yet with much room to grow. Our tendency to have a

toxic behavior and sin must never deter us from striving to be more like Christ. We must pray, repent and ask God to deliver us from sin. Christ calls all of us to excel, to rise above mediocrity, and to mature in every area, becoming like Him.)

Tell those toxic people that if they are not willing to change and submit to God… *"I will not sacrifice to you my life, my mind, my emotions, or my body. These belong to God. I will use them as He tells me to. I will fulfill His plan in my life and I will keep my mind and my emotions clear and calm so that I can hear Him when he speaks to me. God has something for me to do. I have decided I will follow Him. I will not be torn apart by my emotions. I will have His peace and His joy. And if I don't have His peace and His joy, but turmoil and tumult on the inside, then I know I have missed it."*

In 1Corinthians 6:19 states, **"Or do you know that your body is the temple of the Holy Spirit who is in you, whom you have from God and you are not your own."**

Many people say they have the right to do whatever they want with their own bodies' especially toxic controlling people. Although they think that is freedom they are really enslaved to their own desires. Ownership is on their mind and slave mentality to their spouse. But according to scripture we no longer own our bodies. "Bought with a price" refers to slaves purchased as auction. Christ death freed us from sin and bondage, but also obligates us to his service. Toxic people do not own your body Christ does!!

Pray for people, correct people if you can (with the help from a licensed Minister and the Holy Spirit of course), steer them in the right path, sow the seed of God's Word, and let them make their own decisions. Don't tie yourself up emotionally to people who will only destroy you. If they will not do right, let them go. Allow them to make their own choices about how they will live their lives.

A healthy love relationship will always affirm you and build you up. It will move you in a positive direction toward God's plan and purpose for your life. You'll be blessed because of this relationship, not cursed. You'll be warm and safe, not fearful and constantly on an emotional roller coaster.

If you have a problem with an addicted person, go to an Al-Anon meeting or an Alcoholics Anonymous meeting in your area. These groups teach you how to let go of the problem person in your life and get your own life straightened out.

How to recognize abusive person that is Toxic: An abusive person is a controlling person. Where there is control, there is abuse. If you are married to a man/woman who is an abuser, it is more like a father/daughter relationship rather than a relationship of equality and respect. There is nothing that will kill love and passion faster in a relationship then being married to someone who insists on being "one-up" or being in the father or mother role. Who wants to go to bed with their father or mother? Abuse is about power and control.

I will attempt to give an overall portrait of an abuser. Instances and techniques may vary, but most abusers have all or most of these controlling traits. I have seen instances from my life and others, living with an abuser, to illustrate. I also need to state that there are overt abusers and there are covert abusers. Overt abusers come right out and abuse blatantly and boldly. Covert abusers are the worst and the hardest to confront. They do their abusing and controlling in a hidden, manipulative, secretive way. They say one thing with their mouth and appear to be loving and kind, but their actions are controlling and conveying the message that you are stupid and worth nothing in their sight. They manipulate to get their way by getting people to feel sorry for them, making people feel guilty, etc. It's like an evil spirit when someone uses these covert techniques. One of the signs of an abusive person who doesn't recognize they are being abusive and toxic they go and find people who will "pat their flesh" or sympathize with them. To get people to do this, they must manipulate their feelings and get them to believe that they have been unjustly wronged.

So in order for the abuser to get sympathy or consolation from people, they must manipulate them into thinking that they had been unjustly wronged in order to get their "flesh patted" or to get consoled, when they really needs to suffer the consequences of their behavior, which is what will cause them to change. The abuser will call their mother, brother, friends or whoever will listen and tell them untruthful things in order to get them to console them. They will manipulate them to get comforted. The abuser tries to get people to feel sorry for them by sighing, acting hurt and so on. As long as they can find people who will console them instead of let them suffer the consequences of their behavior, they will continue to manipulate people to get them to feel sorry for them so THEY CAN FEEL BETTER and they don't have to take responsibility for their behavior.

This toxic spirit is of a manipulative behavior! Now scripture doesn't specifically quote it's as of witchcraft but it's obviously sinful. While manipulation isn't a form of witchcraft it's a sin in which people manipulate situations, or others seeking glory for themselves rather than being motivated to show God's Glory to others. Now the toxic manipulative behavior can be perceived as witchcraft of trying to manipulating someone. The "feel sorry for me behavior" an "evil spell". One example a person who is manipulative will uses their children against another parent by telling the child, "I guess your mother and I couldn't work things out so I will talk bad about him/her." Or "your daddy doesn't love me so you can't visit him anymore!" A toxic manipulator will tell the children to tell them not to leave to visit their other parent by acting out crying on the floor making the child uncomfortable, scared, guilty and sad because they don't want to disappoint them. Leaving the other parent who didn't cause this helpless for all they wanted to do is have their time with their child during their visitation. That is TOXIC!

They will manipulate a person's emotions to get what they want. That person is a chameleon who changes color depending on who they are with. They will tell you what they think you want to hear in order to protect them. I have seen this type of example give the old "Mr. Repentfull" routine to so many pastors, ministers, bible study leaders, family members and so on, yet they never changes their behavior. A chameleon changes his color according to his surroundings in order to protect himself. A controlling toxic abuser is all about protecting themselves and that is why they control in the first place. They are like a con man, salesman, and can win academy awards for their acting ability. Why even they believe the things they says, yet the behavior never changes and the things they say never line up with the things they do. There is a big gap between the words and walk. That person is unstable and very erratic! In James 1:8 KJV states, *"A double minded man is unstable in all his ways."*

I never forget going to a military counselor with my ex to avoid him getting an Article 15 for hitting me. After the initial consultation the military counselor told my ex that *"he was like a dog that professed undying love and devotion to his family while pissing on their leg!"* He also said that, relationally, things my ex did *"were like making a whole pot of homemade soup. You put in all these good ingredients and then pour in the poison."* Of course my ex didn't see it that way so we stopped going to counseling because in my ex eyes it was destroying "His image" but again a Lesson learned--"You can lead a horse to drink water but you can't make it drink!" (That's another story)

A toxic abusers are often extremely charming and come off as "Mr or Ms. Nice Guy" to those who don't live with them. That is part of that "manipulation" I spoke of earlier. They are fake and a phony! It used to make me sick to my stomach to hear someone say, "What a nice guy (my ex)" was because I knew differently. He had everyone fooled, especially the women! Women fell for this "Mr. Nice Guy" stuff, hook, line and sinker. I did, too, until I married him. I didn't have a clue to his controlling, abusive nature until a week before our wedding. He told me he didn't want to marry me because he wasn't ready to leave the single life. Now I was pregnant with his child but he wanted us to move in together and didn't want to get married. First clue "V8 moment"!! Now don't get me wrong I am not trying to put my ex down as the lowest thing on this earth *(now there was a time in my life I did think that way towards him though)* but there was just something about his behavior that wouldn't go unnoticed. Often times I thought it was me that caused him to act the way he did. Also I did the blame game…blaming myself for EVERY SINGLE that went wrong in that marriage…but it takes two!! I didn't know how to act or respond around him. Walked around tiptoeing on egg shells so to speak! I didn't have anyone to talk to or just to scare to say anything about what was going on in this toxic marriage. Fear crept my heart and many times afraid to do anything wrong because of the reaction that came out from him. There was an image to portray before our friends and family members. No one knew-- I was so consumed and drained. I was lost in my own mess, my own sins, and my desperation of getting out was done by doing things that wasn't godly!

 I reached out for help to the wrong people that cause me to lose my identity! I ended getting involved in a relationship that wasn't conducive to my spiritual walk! I was crying out for help but again I had to portray this image of being the "The perfect minister wife!" Lost, abandoned, used up and abused! Yes I went to church but the church I went to had issues that it was too overwhelming to comprehend openly! (Again that is another story)

This is some of the symptoms of what can happen to you when you are in this type of toxic relationship. The marriage ended and I was a mess—But GOD!!

~More Signs of a Toxic Person: **Using Intimidation:**

Making the family afraid by using looks, actions, gestures, smashing things, destroying property, abusing pets, displaying weapons. That person uses intimidation to glare at them and have them fear them in order to cause them to behave, especially around other people. That way they wouldn't have to correct them in public. I have seen and witness a toxic person that would pound his fist on things when he couldn't get that person to do what he wanted. For ex: A toxic person who has a daughter and if she wasn't doing her homework right, they would scream at the top of their lungs at her, lecturer her and pound on things or throw things. Another example: The intimidator toxic parent will sit in a car in the garage lecturing their 12 year old child, but the child will tune them out as teenagers often do. If that parent couldn't control her if she wasn't listening to him. That parent will become frustrated that she wasn't listening and loses control of the situation and will begin to hit or punch. Now there is a better way to handle your child without violence but when a toxic parent who is not in control of himself they would go to this drastic measure to gain control!!

The spirit of intimidation of the abuser portrays as innocent when around people. They like to be around people who are unstable and unsure. So they can discredit them and make that person feel inferior. This is an isolation technique that abusers use to isolate their family from anyone who would help them. This cuts the family off from neighbors, family, friends, pastors, or anyone who may offer support to the abuser's family or his victims. Often this would make anyone feel abandon by God and others. You will feel like no one would listen to you, believe you or help you because of the power that person has over you by intimidation. There will be a great disconnect in your spirit.

This kind of mental and emotional control is designed to isolate you and cut you off from anyone who would help you or intervene. The abuser would have everyone turn against you with their lies. People won't look at you or acknowledge you. Especially in the church if there isn't a spirit of discernment operating the members will fall into the trap of the abuser intimidation. They will feel lead to help the abuser because of the lies they told about you and even "church members" become bold enough to go up to the abuser and pat them on the shoulder in front of you and say, *"We'll get through this together. Just hang in there."* Now you ask how I know this really happens. We'll let me tell you I am witness to it all. This has happened to me several times to a point I thought I was going crazy. Or actually causing that person to react this way towards me which gave the excuse to continue it!! I was abandoned by anyone in a position of authority to help me. The abuse I felt had controlled me in public and on the way to church. We always had to "look good" and appear happy so that no one approached him because "I looked depressed or not happy" and as head of the household, it will appear that the spouse must be doing something wrong.

Nothing I did was right. He always has a better way of doing things and if I didn't do things his way or take his advice, he uses the intimidation methods of control or he resorts to shaming and belittling me. I couldn't even clean the house right in our home in his eyesight. He saw a better way to do it and insisted on "helping" me do it a better way. When you are always being "fixed", "helped" and "controlled", the constant unspoken relational message you keep getting is *"You are stupid, incapable, and incompetent. You can't do anything right. I am smarter, better and above you in all ways."* It is a form of putting others down so that you can feel better about yourself.

Anyway, a toxic person who uses their intimidation power will thrown things, pounded their fist on things and used glares and gestures to cause their family to fear them in order to control them, yet they can't understand why they are feared. When you throw things, pound your fist, etc. the unspoken message that is being communicated loud and clear is: "This could or will be you I am hitting next if you don't do what I want!" (Pretty scary huh?—Yeah I know!)

After divorce papers had been filed and I was no longer staying in the home. What my ex would do to continue the control process he would call my job and tell everyone that I was cheating on him and also sent emails to supervisors in each department. He called my realtor of the apartment I stayed in one time threatening them if they didn't revoke the rental agreement he will file charges against them. He had me followed. He knew my every move. Even though we weren't living together as husband and wife he still felt the need to control me. Yes I reached out of marriage to a male companion which in every aspect was WRONG!! But there was no excuse from my ex to treat me this way!!

I started to see this type of behavior as a deep impact on our children. They had a hard time talking to their dad because of the fear of saying things wrong or doing something wrong in his presence when they were young. Also they were having struggles talking to me because they didn't understand what was going on…they hated the both of us and loves us at the same time! One of my daughters had speech impairment behind it all…she use to flinch and stutter a lot when she was small.

One time my daughter didn't like the vegetables that was fixed for her and refused to swallow it. She held it in her mouth (as all children do when they don't like certain foods) but that made my ex husband very angry and he disciplined her to point that scared me. I begged him to stop whipping her and let her throw the food away not every child likes what we like as I tried to explain to him. He didn't let up until he realized the whelps that he put on her was turning black and blue. I never told my daughter about this incident because she was very young but her fear of her dad had everything to do with her speech impairment!!

When she was old enough she asked me why she stuttered so much…. I told her it was the medicine that I took when I was pregnant with her. (I know she will read this and I hope she forgives me for withholding this information from her) I didn't want to cause any anger between her and her dad by telling the truth. I wish I did though because as she gotten older there were some deep issues and unresolved anguish that lay dormant in her mind and heart towards me and her dad. For years, I blamed myself because of the failure of my marriage and not able to have a healthy marriage like I dreamed!!

My children felt that I wasn't there to protect them from all the abandonment, fear, intimidation, rejection, and manipulation that were roaming in our home. We (my ex and I) became toxic to our children of what they saw and heard in the home. (For that I regret and I asked all of them to forgive me.)

Listen all, you too can become toxic to your children if you don't recognize the signs. Be careful and don't fall in the devils trap.

Thanks be to God… all my children are healed and no longer bound by what happened between their parents. Yes we still have some issues but who doesn't? Honestly, we all can move forward in our lives and learn from the lessons that were presented to us and making sure it doesn't become "Generational Curse In Jesus Name!" We bind it!!! Amen!

Using Emotional Abuse: *Putting family members down, making them feel bad about themselves, calling them names, making them think they are crazy, playing mind games, humiliating them, making them feel guilty.*

A toxic abuser is a master at these. By constantly, "fixing and helping!" Putting family members down and by ruining their self esteem and making them dependent on them in an unhealthy way. I remember in my youth my mom told me that I was ugly and wished I wasn't born. She would always say things like "why can't I be smart like my little brother!" I mean I wasn't the brightest person but I wasn't dumb either! I just wasn't as smart as my brother and at times I use to be jealous of him. The results of him being so smart my mom and him would have deep conversations and a lot of fun together. I wanted to have that type of relationship with my mom but it was no avail.

My dad was in the home but very rarely said anything. He was a quiet person and my mom ran the home! As you can say "she wore the pants". Disciplinary came from mom and I can count on both of my hands where my dad disciplined me. Another time, I use to have problems with acne as a teenager and instead of my mom showing how to keep my skin clean and healthy she would throw facial cream/acne medication at me and say *"wash your face for you look like a road map!"* I cried each time she said that to me and for that I had self esteem issues. I thought I wasn't pretty, just ugly and worthless. I wouldn't even look in a mirror. I felt like the ugly duckling in the story book. Everyday more seeds of toxic were planted in me. Nothing I did measured up! She knew what to do to pull me to my lowest point.

It got so bad that I accepted and believed what was told to me. She knew I was depended on my mom because I was still a teenager and not old enough to be on my own. With that said I was dependence on my mom... waiting to hear the negativity from her every day. My mom would have a way of telling me things that would be believable because I was vulnerable for affection. She would say things like *"you will never make it and you will never be anything!" "You are so stupid you will never measure up to anyone!"* I was so impressionable and I fed into her lies. One time I will never forget this incident from my brother (I am not even sure if he remembers this) but he walked in my bedroom just in the nick of time where I was ready to take my life! I had a razor blade in my hand, ready to cut my wrist for I was emotional wreck! I was crying and saying to myself *"why should I stay in this world when no one wants me or love me?!"* My brother said to me *"Hey Marsh, what are you doing… are you okay?"* If he didn't walk in… my destiny would been aborted and my mom speaking those negative toxic words in my life would have manifested. (Thank you God, for speaking to my brother.) Since that wakeup call from God using my brother a couple months later at the age of 18, I left home because of the toxic environment I was living in. So you ask do I forgive my mom for doing and saying the toxic words ….YES! Check out my book, "Broken to Forgive When Other's Don't!"

So to say, a toxic abuser resorts to shaming others. Especially, when the people they supposed to care about don't think, feel, or want the same things they do. If you want to do something for yourself and the toxic abuser doesn't, they will go into trying to convince you to see things their way and they will debate you. If that doesn't work, they will shame you in public or in secret and discard your feelings, thoughts, wants and needs by explaining them away with his/her reasoning and rationale. The constant unspoken message is *"You have no reason to 'feel, think, need or want' the things you do because........"* They will make you feel like a bad person for feeling or wanting what you do. They rarely say yes to anything when asked and many times when you asked for things in your marriage and they will say they'll do them and then conveniently forgets and never does them. This is passive/aggressive behavior.

As you can see there are many traits of toxic behavior in a person. It can lead to many behavioral problems within them and sometimes it could be intentional or not intentional. Please don't take this type of behavior passively but seriously!! Get help immediately and get out!

If you are not careful this toxic behavior in that person could result in more controlling attitude. They will act like you are needed their "permission" for everything and anything in your life. It is their way or no way. If you think, feel, want or need something that they have judged that you "shouldn't" because of their reasoning or rationale, they will negate you and emotionally abuse you by shaming you, belittling you, calling you names, etc. Abusers want to tell you what to think, feel, look like, want and generally dictate who you are as a person. You become who they want you to be. He used to say, "God knew I needed an attractive wife" and if I wanted to get my hair cut, he would follow me around, telling me how much he liked my hair now (covert manipulation). He never told me this at other times. Only if he felt I may cut my hair in a style he didn't like. This was his way of trying to stop me from keeping my hair appointment. I was always the **"trophy wife"** that validated his manhood and reflected on what others thought of him and his masculinity. He uses to call me his "toy" and if anyone messes with his toys he will hurt them. I wasn't the type of wife according to Proverbs 31 but a slave to his mind games and manipulation. Thank goodness for my dear friend Marry Smith (with the two R's Wink…Wink!) for introducing this wonderful team of Social workers who help me get out of this ordeal. If it wasn't for

Marry to see that her friend was in trouble I think I would have stayed in that marriage today. Also I wouldn't have met my wonderful husband Jay. Thank you Marry love you girl!

Using Isolation

Controlling what she does, who she sees and talks to, what she reads, where she goes, limiting her outside involvement, using jealousy to justify actions these are signs of Isolation! I had a close friend who was going through mental and physical abuse tell me when her husband had found out that she went to someone outside the family for help, like a pastor, bible study leader, etc., it would result in physical abuse. Her husband shoves her around and even punched her after finding out that she went to a Pastor for help. My heart went out to her immediately!! You never know what a person is going through especially behind a smile! My friend told me that her ex would walk in the house to bring intimidation to her all the time. He would badger her and following her around to bring fear in her heart. I told her to get out because she wasn't safe regardless how many times he asked her forgiveness. One time I was invited to her home just to have some coffee. When I rang the door bell I saw something that had me grasping for air! I saw my friend husband shoved her hard up against the dresser and started choking her! I banged on the door and fiercely rang the door bell until she came to the door. Of course her eyes were bloodshot and her voice was quivering from crying. I told her that I was going to call the police but she cried and beg me not to. I cried in fear for her because I wanted so badly for her to seek help and to leave that toxic environment! I saw the choke marks on her throat but again she begged me not to call and that he promised her that he would change! Listen how many of you all know that is NOT always the case! An abuser who doesn't seek help will always be an abuser no matter what! PLEASE CALL THE POLICE!! DON'T ALLOW THAT TO CONTINUE!!

Please know as you read this that person who is the abuser is a TOXIC person. Any abuser will tell neighbors, friends or anyone else that has heard even a small portion of what goes on in their family, that they are the victim and the person whom they are causing harm to that they are "unstable, or mental or unfaithful". Passing the blame and to appear innocent. Having everyone feel sorry for them in all in all they are the ones causing the harm. Isn't that what the devil does? "Being the accuser of the brethren!"

Minimizing, Denying and Blaming

light of the abuse and not taking her concerns about it seriously, saying the abuse didn't happen, shifting responsibility for abusive behavior, saying she caused it, provoked it, etc.

Minimizing, denying, blaming, rationalizing, justifying, explaining, giving your intent, are all forms of denial. This is used so that the toxic abuser does not have to look at or accept responsibility for his or her behavior and how it affects others. It actually gives them permission to continue their controlling, hurtful behavior. It is a defending technique and the abuser is all about self defense. *Example: He has been involved in karate since he was 15 or 16 years old up until he was 30 years old. He is a third degree black belt in karate and he is drenched in self defense. Talk about a mental stronghold!!! Many of his relational/emotional techniques are block/blow techniques. He will block the incoming confrontation about his hurtful behavior with rationalizing, justifying, explaining, etc. and then deliver a shaming accusatory blow to you to put you down to take the focus off himself. He would rather change your feelings about his behavior then accept responsibility for his behavior.*

An abuser believes they are well-intentioned many times and has the interest of the victim at heart and wants the best for them. The end justifies the means. They will cross lines and boundaries in order to "help or fix" their loved ones because they think they know what is best for them and they don't respect their identity and boundaries. He/she looks down upon them and their abilities and he/she places themselves above them. They are incapable, unable, not as smart as, etc. so he/she must help them. This is why he/she gives their intentions to justify their behavior and this is why he/she doesn't see their behavior as abusive.

The abuser "loves" their family and thinks is doing what is best for them. The abuser gives their "good, loving" intentions most of the time when they are confronted with their abusive behavior. Because he/she thinks that they are doing things out of "love", he/she doesn't see it as hurtful and abusive. Many times they do not accept your feelings of hurt because he/she is "well intentioned" and therefore you have no reason to feel the way you do. *Ex: The abuser molests their daughter or son because he/she loved them and wanted her/him to allow us to intervene in a situation at school and he/she couldn't do that if they tune him out and wouldn't listen. An abusive person's love really amounts to fear and because they are afraid of the outcome of a situation, they try to control it and they will violate physical, emotional, mental, and sexual boundaries in order to do this.*

When a person goes through a toxic behavior of the abuser they develops a boundary which is an invisible line that determines where one person stops and another person begins. We see boundaries with our neighbors. There is a line where our property stops and theirs begins. The same is true with countries, personal body space, etc. There are also emotional and psychological boundaries as well. This is a line that determines where one person stops and the other begins. To cross a boundary against another person's will constitutes abuse and this is why Jesus said, "If your brother trespasses against you, rebuke him. How do you know if you have been trespassed against if you don't even know where the boundary or line is? Jesus observes our boundaries and expects us to observe and respect others. Abusive, controlling people do not respect, observe and know about boundaries. They want to tell you what to think, what to feel, what to want, who to be, what to look like, smell like and they want to determine who you are and what your identity is. You lose your identity when living with an abusive, controlling, shamer.

I know that I did for part of my life. I let other people tell me what to think, feel, want, look like and so on. I let other people determine who I was so that I could be loved and accepted. Problem is, with these people, you never feel loved or accepted. Nothing you do is ever good enough. They never see or acknowledge anything good you've done or any accomplishments you have made. They are quick to point out your faults, failures, shortcomings and things you don't do as well as they do. They are quick to help you or fix you and inform you that there is something wrong with you and that you don't measure up. I felt that so many times with my parents, siblings, and "so called" friends. They do not accept your feelings, wants, needs or thoughts. They rationalize them away, like you don't exist, and in their mind you don't because you don't have a good reason to feel, want, need or think the things you do.

Feelings are not right or wrong. To label a feeling as wrong is judging and nobody has any right to tell or determine what another person should feel, need, want, etc. To do so is crossing an emotional boundary and it is emotional abuse. We have no right to tell another how something should be that belongs to them. This is like telling your neighbor how their lawn, home or children should be. Their property is not yours to determine how it should be. To do so is crossing a line or a boundary. It is violating the other person's property either physically, emotionally, psychologically, or sexually. To touch something that is not yours to touch without the other person's permission is called abuse. We can touch it with our hands, a weapon, our words, actions, etc. The part that makes up you as an individual is: your feelings, wants, needs, thoughts, appearance, etc. To not accept these things is to not accept you. A person is not what they do. Who a person is comes from their wants, needs, desires, thoughts, feelings, etc. This is what makes you who you are and this is what makes you an individual. Controllers use the same brainwashing techniques on their families as they do on prisoners of war or that they do in cults. They explain away or rationalize away your feelings, needs, wants, thoughts and so on. They don't accept them. They try to fix and change them and then shame you for them if their attempts to rationalize and convince you fail. In negating your feelings, needs, thoughts, wants, etc., they are negating you and not accepting you as a person. They put you down for not feeling, thinking, needing or wanting the same things they do or for not being like them. You lose your identity and become a clone of them. The problem is that just because they explain away your feelings, doesn't make your feelings go away. You just deny and repress your feelings, needs, wants, thoughts, etc. You become numb, emotionally frozen and dead inside, which is the kind of mother my kids had for a number of years, or you get angry and start setting boundaries with abusive, controlling, boundary bashing people. talking about abuse and how it correlates to Toxic relationships?! Well in my own personal opinion it all wraps up to being toxic. Anyone who makes you feel inferior, controls, manipulates and suffocates you to prevent you to be all God created you to be is toxic. I have experience it, I lived it, and I know it. I can't share something that I haven't experienced. That is just like having a test and never ever had a book to read or study from. In order to share a testimony you must have a test. In 1 Peter 4:12-19 KJV states, *"Beloved, think it not strange concerning the fiery trial which is to try you, as though some strange thing happened unto you: But rejoice, inasmuch as ye are partakers of Christ's sufferings; that, when his glory shall be revealed, ye may be glad also with exceeding joy. If ye be reproached for the name of Christ, happy are ye; for the spirit of glory and of God resteth upon you: on their part he is evil spoken of, but on your part he is glorified. But let none of you suffer as a murderer, or as a thief, or as an evildoer, or as a busybody in other men's matters. Yet if any man suffer as a Christian, let him not be ashamed; but let him glorify God on this behalf. For the time is come that judgment must begin at the house of God: and if it first begin at us, what shall the end be of them that obey not the gospel of God? And if the righteous scarcely be saved, where shall the ungodly and the sinner appear? Wherefore let them that suffer according to the will of God commit the keeping of their souls to him in well doing, as unto a faithful Creator."* God never told His children they would not have problems and trial in this life. He did promise to "never leave us or forsake us" and to be by our side through whatever comes our way whether it is good things or difficulties.

Abuse of Power:

During the Iraq/Kuwait Gulf war, I kept praying and asking God why it was that people thought they could do this. What makes people think that they can invade the boundary or border of another and think that was o.k? I had learned about boundaries in relationships and I had tried to establish boundaries in my relationships with controlling people, only to be physically abused and shamed all the more because they couldn't control and manipulate me anymore the way they were used to. The more control a controller loses, the more insecure and angry he becomes. Anyway, I had just prayed this prayer or asked this question of God one day in frustration. I turned on CNN News and they were covering the Iraq/Kuwait war. Saddam was invading the physical boundary and border of a neighbor in an effort to take over. In the news, they were interviewing Iraqis and asking them why they thought they could take over Kuwait. Each Iraqi had the same answer, "Because Kuwait belongs to us." What causes someone to border bash or cross boundaries of another person is because they believe they own them. It is a matter of possession and ownership. You are a thing, not a person. What you want and need do not count. God answered my questions within ten minutes after I prayed it. The attitude is the same. This is why abusers and controllers don't necessarily do it to others outside their family. They do it to those "they own" or those "within their possession" or control. You amount to their property. They refer to you as "my wife", "my family" and so on and they do not mention your name because giving you a name individualizes and personalizes you.

Anyway, back to denial, through blaming, minimizing, rationalizing, explaining, etc. There is a saying that goes, "If you don't admit it, you won't quit it." This is also scriptural. In 1 John 1:9 states, *"If we confess our sins, He is faithful and just to forgive us our sins and to cleanse us from all unrighteousness."* Until you acknowledge and accept responsibility for your behavior and what it causes in others and in your relationships, your behavior won't change. As long as you have a good reason for doing what you did, and you are deceived enough to believe that because your intention was good, the behavior and results of it couldn't be bad, and as long as you are deceived enough to believe that someone else caused you to behave the way you do because they "provoked it", then you will never change. I love this verse. Here's what the Word says:

"Who Himself (Jesus) bore our sins in his own body on the tree, that we, having died to sins, might live for righteousness—by whose stripes we were healed." (1 Peter 2:24 NKJV)

It's such a powerful, yet simple truth. If we blow it, if we sin, God says to us—don't cover it up. Just admit it and then quit it—don't do it again. But if you slip and repeat it, just run back to 1 John 1:9 and bring it to the Lord because He is faithful and just to forgive. I know it's hard to believe that our God is this forgiving, but it's true, He is. When people do us wrong, when they blow it, we tend to hold it over them, but not God—He takes it away! It's the very reason that Jesus went to the cross. He went there to pay for our sins, to be punished on our behalf. That means God has no need to punish you for your sins, because He laid them all on Jesus.

I remember a time when I called a certain Minister's wife to explain what was going on and she told me that I provoked my spouse to be physically violent and abusive towards me. She simply said that I deserve everything that had happened to me. It was hurtful words coming from someone whom I respected, trusted and admired. I didn't imagine that those words would have uttered out of the mouth of a "woman of God!"

Tell me, what is a good reason to physically abuse your spouse? I also had gone to a close family male friend about what was going on in our home. I wanted a male Christian to hold him accountable and step in because the verbal and mental abuse wasn't changing, he was only getting worse. Yes I have reached out to another male for companionship in which that was wrong (Read my book "Broken to Forgive When Others Don't explaining more about it) But no one--not matter who they are Male or Female deserves to be abused! After being verbally badgered, I told him about himself. He exploded and started saying how he would go to them and the pastor and tell them all kinds of stuff about me so that I would not be believed. He laughed at me to make me feel helpless and alone. This is an "Isolation" technique that we talked about earlier. This cuts the woman off from any support, emotionally or otherwise, that she could receive. As long as she is isolated, he can continue to control. If she receives help, support and the things she needs, he loses control and now is accountable to others.

So to speak, when my ex spouse told me that he was going to do this, I yelled at him to stop. Then he started the abusive laughing and he began verbally abusing me. He said he felt "betrayed". He goes and tells people that I was the one who cheated and betrayed him that is why we are in the condition that we were in. I was "unstable, mental" and so on and so forth and he is the one who feels "betrayed". I'm suppose to worry about him feeling "betrayed" because I'm going to someone outside the family for help so that an end can be put to all this control and abuse because he will not accept responsibility for his behavior and what it causes. NOTE: The abuser tries to change your feelings and thoughts regarding his behavior. That way he doesn't have to change and accept responsibility for what he does.

Here is another example: The abuser has a good excuse, explanation, reason or whatever for everything he is confronted on. If he looks at another woman, it is your fault because you would not make eye contact with him, or he wasn't looking at her with the "intent" to lust and so on and so on. The abuser is a womanizer. He will look or follow woman or young attractive women in your presence, no matter how much you have asked him not to. It has cost him physical intimacy with you because you won't be intimate with someone who has so little regard for you, your marriage or your feelings. This isn't healthy and it's very toxic! Seek help! There is defiantly something wrong with this picture!

I know you all may be wondering why this chapter is longer than the rest well because a lot of people today and being deceived into thinking that it's okay to be a toxic person or the person receiving the toxic. Well I am coming to tell you that the devil is a LIAR! BE FREE IN JESUS NAME AND GET OUT!!!

CHAPTER THREE

~Protect Your Self Esteem~
Take Your Power Back!

I thank God for this chapter because for this topic *protect your self esteem and also taking your power back* that was something that only God had to heal. There were a lot of people I had allowed to come in my life to unload hatred, bitterness, frustration, grudges, anguish, hostility and pain. *I was told that I wouldn't make it in life. I wouldn't find a good husband! No one was better but them! I would be searching for happiness or someone like them because of the failed marriage that person felt that they were the only one for me—no one else!! Who can control my action and I will fail on my next marriage! I will never excel or advance in my career because I don't have a college degree!* Just toxic venom being released in my spirit!

The venom that was released in my spirit was so toxic that I didn't realize the weight of the baggage in my life was way too much for me to bear. My health became affected where I stayed sick all the time; my spiritual walk with God was limited because I wasn't communing with Him and didn't want any parts of God because of the bitterness I felt! My family relationship (siblings and parents) was in havoc because I was so worried about what they thought of me, trying to keep the relationship together in my family or worrying why they weren't communicating with me! I noticed that I had a lot of back pain, headaches, sleepless nights and stress in my life. At times I was so drained and didn't want to get up from bed where I was so depressed and anxious all the time.

What happens if the toxic person is your siblings or parents? Wow.... this is a touchy subject and yes it's quite painful! I didn't want to respond about this or even elaborate on this matter simply because I knew how this may be misinterpret or cause hard feelings towards my intermediate family members but I learned if you don't deal with it there is no way you can get help from it! For years I battled with this issue! I thought I was the problem! I searched, asked, meditated, asked again, sought counseling and even took the blame for not doing anything to my immediate family member!

I was misunderstood, lied upon, used, abused, abandoned, and hated! I even did what the word of God says, *"If you have an ought against the person (even though it wasn't me!) go to them* (Matthew 18:15) I was told that they wished I wasn't born!" Or that "you are so ugly and I wish you weren't my child!" As a child those words are powerful especially coming from someone you loved and trusted! They can cut you to the core! So you end up growing up with a complex about yourself! Insecurity settles in! Believing those words that were told to you by your *"trusted family member"*! And so self pity and bitterness takes root! I did things as a child that wasn't pleasing to my parents to gain attention but you know that still didn't faze or move them. *This was painful writing this but I know that God is healing me through this and I know I am free* in Jesus name! I want to be transparent before my Heavenly Father with no hidden baggage. Thank you Jesus!

Hey I'm not saying during my younger years I was a perfect child because I wasn't! I've done some things that were unforgivable but by Gods grace and mercy I was forgiven! (Romans 8:1NKJV, **"There is therefore now no condemnation to them which are in Christ Jesus, who walk not after the flesh, but after the Spirit."**) I am still pursuing the things of God and trying to walk the straight and narrow way with His guidance (Matthew 7:14 NKJV, **"Because narrow is the gate and difficult is the way which leads to life, and there are few who find it."**) but let's be real about this okay everyone! It was hard going through this life without coming to the realization that I was in Christ Jesus! If it wasn't for Him I wouldn't realize that I was *"Fearfully and wonderfully made!"* Psalms 139:14!

During those dark times in my teenage to early adult hood life I was so lonely and I couldn't rely on my siblings for aide simply because they were only doing what my parents told them to do when they were younger which was caused by manipulation and control. Now things have changed since we are older but there are still some residues left. I am not saying that every sibling relationship is "perfect" but when there is no structure or balance on handling toxic family member then the revolving door remains open.

A lot of people didn't know what was going on in my parents' home and thought we were "The perfect family" but how many know that there isn't no perfect family in the eye sight of God! Hey please get me wrong I am not here to bash my family or to embarrass anyone or cause shame on the family name! All I am trying to do is to expose the devils ugly schemes and tactics on families and the toxic venom he tries to seep in! John 10:10 NIV, ***"The thief comes only to steal and kill and destroy; I have come that they may have life, and have it to the full."*** I know many of you are wondering are we on talking terms i.e. speaking of my parents and siblings? Well as painfully it may be ….the answer is "NO! My heart goes out to them DAILY and I constantly pray and think of them often but in Gods own timing I believe HIS healing process will take place! Do I forgive my parents and siblings you ask? Most definitely! You ask why the communication is not where it should be. Well for years I guess I was the one always trying to gain the affection and communicable relationship. But after the switching off and on I guess I got pretty tired of being bounced off or ignored—I realized that I can't force anyone to speak or be in relationship with me if they don't want it. I had to learn that the hard way!! I was upset for years at God wondering why this process is taking forever or why none of my family members wanted to be apart in my life. I felt ashamed and even embarrassed when people come to me asking me *"how my parents doing or how is my sister or brother doing or you are twin wow tell me about her?"* I didn't want to lie to them so I just simply say, *"I wish I knew"!* I normally receive a blank look stare for them but I don't allow that to damper me or discourage me any longer. Even though I longed for the relationship to be stable and to be with them… I just had enough of it all and God it all over to God!!!

One day I read in Psalm 27:10 **"When my father and my mother forsake me, then the LORD will take me up."** That was the hard part for me in letting go! Even though I love my parents and siblings but I had to let go and let God! I learned that the love of God is stronger and more certain than even that of a father or mother, or siblings since he will never forsake his people. Though every other tie that binds heart to heart should dissolve, this will remain; though a case might occur in which we could not be sure of the love that naturally springs out of the tenderest earthly relationships, yet we can always confide in His love. So I asked God to forgive me for the wrong thinking and I released my parents and siblings to him! Whew…what a weight lifted!

I can recall a movie I watched, [8]"What's Love Got To Do With It!" In this film it was about a singer name Tina Turner and how she rose to stardom with her abusive husband Ike Turner and how she gained the courage to break free! She was a shy little country girl singing with a church choir. She had a natural talent and it's a gift that will save her from poverty and obscurity. It also turned her into the world-famous musical dynamo known as Tina Turner, and places her in the clutches of a smooth-talking Svengali named Ike.

In less confessional times, the tale of Ike Turner's stormy, violent relationship with his long-abused wife Tina and star attraction might not have had the makings of a Hollywood biography. Forced into show business servitude no matter how sick or exhausted she might be, Tina Turner suffered years of vicious beatings, marital infidelities and other indignities. It took vast reserves of courage for her to break free.

Early in the story, when Anna Mae (a.k.a Tina Turner) has newly moved to St. Louis to be with the mother who had abandoned her in childhood, Ike is seen as a veritable human magnet. Locally famous as both a bandleader and a ladies' man, Ike gives Tina her first chance to perform onstage, then marvels in true "Star Is Born" fashion at her show-stopping talent. This scene, a nicely staged version of the standard crowd-pleaser, constitutes almost the only point in the story at which Ike displays an unselfish appreciation of what Tina can do.

Smiling, cajoling and sweet-talking his way through the first part of the story, Ike's considerable acumen makes him understand just how Tina should dress, sing and move to best effect, and Tina obligingly becomes his creature.

Under the influence of drugs, Ike becomes a desperate, jive-talking mess, venting his jealousy of Tina's success in excruciating ways. The film retains its fundamentally glossy tone despite the fact that Ike is seen beating Tina with his boot in a limousine, raping her during a domestic quarrel, blackening her eye before a performance and forcing her to leave her hospital bed when she says she's too weak to work. It understands that the dream of success that intoxicated Ike somehow damaged him as badly as it hurt those around him. This is a perfect example of a toxic person (Ike) and person breaking free (Tina Turner). Even though I don't believe in her religious belief but I do applaud her effort of breaking free from the one person whom she loved and trusted with her life/career. She broke free from being damaged goods, she broke free of the control mind games, and she broke free of verbal, mental, physical, she broke free from venom husband name calling and sexual abuse! Tina Turner recognized and said *"that if I don't leave this man and this environment it might just kill me"* and her eyes was opened to see she was in a toxic relationship!

Now I know I heard a lot of people asking me or others, *"Why won't they just leave that person?"* Or *"What is taking them so long to recognize the signs?"* Or *"How long will it take when you say enough is enough?"* Unless you have been through this-- you will never understand the impact of controlling toxic spirit on someone's mind! It's like someone putting a spell on you and you can't get out or better yet you are caught in big spider's web nest and everywhere you turn clouds of web are in your way. Until you seek help and are strong enough to escape you will continue staying in that situation or get involve with the same cycle of manipulating toxic spirit with another person.

There are several scriptures that deal with denial: In John 3:19 states, **"Some men love darkness rather than light and will not come to the light that their deeds can be reproved that they were wrought in darkness."** Light and Truth expose darkness, or hold the mirror up to someone's behavior. A person who explains, rationalizes, justifies, minimizes, gives his intent and so on do not want to see the truth and they want to remain in their deceived state of darkness. They would rather smash the mirror, than see their true reflection.

In Proverbs 28:13 states, *"A man who covers his sin will not prosper."* How does a man cover or hide his sin? Through denial, explaining, minimizing, rationalizing, giving his intent, blaming, etc. Denial, explaining, rationalizing, minimizing, giving intent, blaming, etc. all keep us in darkness and keep us from seeing reality. If the sinner do not acknowledge his sins; if he cover and excuse them, and refuse to come to the light of God's word and Spirit, lest his deeds should be reproved, he shall find no salvation. God will never admit a sinful, unhumbled soul, into his kingdom. But if he confesses his sin, with a penitent and broken heart, and, by forsaking every evil way, give this proof that he feels his own sore, and the plague of his heart, and then he shall have mercy.

Another scripture that comes to mind is in Isaiah 5:20 that states, *"Woe to them who call evil, good?"* How do we call evil, good? By having a good explanation, rationalization, intent for what we did. Want to know why Jesus never defended Himself? It crosses an emotional boundary and equals abuse. You can never resolve anything or be reconciled to anyone, even God, if you defend yourself by denying your behavior, give explanations for your behavior, rationalize your behavior, minimize your behavior, give your good intentions or blame someone else. When you defend yourself using these techniques or even have a defensive attitude, you are closed to anything that anyone else has to say. You are intent on being heard and "understood" and you are not open minded or willing to hear and understand. You are protecting yourself and your heart at someone else's expense. Jesus never did anything for Himself at anyone else's expense.

When a person explains, rationalizes, justifies and gives their intent, they are focused on themselves and what you are thinking of them, not on other people and relieving their pain. They are all about themselves. To defend yourself means that you negate someone else's feelings and abuse them emotionally. Here is a GREAT EXAMPLE: Even when others were wrong and Jesus was right and He, of all people, could have justifiably defended Himself, He chose not to out of love for other people. He was focused on them and their needs and not His own, even when His very life was threatened. Jesus said in Luke 23:34NIV, *"Father, forgive them, for they do not know what they are doing." And they divided up his clothes by casting lots*. The word "betray" in the bible means to protect yourself at someone else's expense. When we defend ourselves that is what we are doing. We are more concerned with ourselves and our own needs, than we are about someone else's and walking in love toward them. We sure won't be listening to them with an open heart seeking resolution and reconciliation. The bible says that in end times mother will betray daughter and sons will betray fathers. (Luke 12:53 NIV states, *"They will be divided, father against son and son against father, mother against daughter and daughter against mother, mother-in-law against daughter-in-law and daughter-in-law against mother-in-law.";* Matthew 10:21 NIV states, *"Brother will betray brother to death, and a father his child; children will rebel against their parents and have them put to death."* and Micah 7:6 NIV states, *"For a son dishonors his father, a daughter rises up against her mother, a daughter-in-law against her mother-in-law-- a man's enemies are the members of his own household."*) People will be seeking to protect themselves and their own interests and hearts at the expense of others, especially other family members, in end times. (Matthew 10:35 NIV states, *"For I have come to turn a man against his father, a daughter against her mother, a daughter-in-law against her mother-in-*

law")This is seen today. That is why Jesus never defended Himself. He trusted the Father to vindicate Him—again I said "He trusted the Father to vindicate HIM!!" For that we must have that same faith and trust in Our Heavenly Father to vindicate us as well.

If He knew He was wrongly accused, then He believed that God the Father would vindicate Him. Because He believed this, He didn't have to vindicate Himself by defending. A person, who truly believes in his heart that God will vindicate him, doesn't vindicate himself by defending. In Psalm 54:1-7 speaks about this, *"Save me, O God, by your name; vindicate me by your might. Hear my prayer, O God; listen to the words of my mouth. Strangers are attacking me; ruthless men seek my life-- men without regard for God. "Selah" Surely God is my help; the Lord is the one who sustains me. Let evil recoil on those who slander me; in your faithfulness destroy them. I will sacrifice a freewill offering to you; I will praise your name, O LORD, for it is good. For he has delivered me from all my troubles, and my eyes have looked in triumph on my foes."*

What a person does, says what they believe in their heart, even though they may say the opposite with their mouth. The abuser says all kinds of things, but his actions do not line up with his words. Luke 6:45NIV states, *"The good man brings good things out of the good stored up in his heart, and the evil man brings evil things out of the evil stored up in his heart. For out of the overflow of his heart his mouth speaks."* If you believe that someone is capable of doing something or handling something themselves because they are capable (like the toxic abuser says) then you don't keep trying to fix, help, and control and do things for them. If a person truly believes something in their heart, their actions will line up. If they don't, there is deception within that person. You have a deceived toxic person on your hands.

Many people claim to be Christians and say that they believe in their heart, yet their actions don't line up and result in obedience and works. That is why James says: *"Can such a faith save you?"* (James 1:21-22) Basically, James is saying that you are deceived. That is not saving faith. To these kinds of people Jesus states in Luke 6:46, *"Why do you call me Lord, Lord and do not the things that I say."* Basically, this is a person who is deceived and he calls Jesus, Lord and Savior, when Jesus does not have Lordship over his life. The fruit of the spirit is not operating in his or her life (Fruit of spirit is: Love, Gentleness, Peace, Faithfulness, Joy, Goodness, Patience, Self-control and Kindness.

In the book "⁶Changes That Heal" by Dr. Henry Cloud, he talks about how denial comes from a person having an "Ideal Self". This is an image they have of themselves as they would ideally be. This is a fantasy. It is not reality. A person sees himself as being a certain way and when you confront him with reality, the denial comes and you get all the defending, denial, explaining, justifying, minimizing, good intents, etc. If you confront a person who has this ideal image of themselves, and, if what you confront them with doesn't line up with their false, but ideal, image of themselves which they perceive as real because they are deceived, then they don't accept what you confront them with because it *"doesn't fit"*. *"It isn't me, so you must be wrong."* They don't see themselves as the person who would do what you just confronted them with. Their actions don't line up with their words and when you point out the discrepancies, you get the denial..

Jesus exposed the discrepancies as He ministered to deceived people to bring them to salvation and into the truth. They were deceived and thought they were already there. These people thought they were something they were not and they truly believed what they thought and they would have passed a lie detector test. That is why the bible says in Jeremiah 17:9, *"that our hearts are wicked and deceitful above all things."*

We are blind to what is truly in our hearts and we need our hearts exposed to us and searched out and Jesus did this. The people, who love darkness rather than light, won't like it when their hearts or true motives are exposed. They will try to remain in the darkness through their defending and denial. They want to continue to believe the false ideal of themselves than to see themselves and their actions in light of reality and truth.

Example: The story of the rich young ruler (in Matthew 19:16-22), this rich young ruler had heard Jesus preach and watched Him perform miracles. He came to Jesus one day and said, *"Good master, what I must do to inherit eternal life?"* Jesus replied, *"Why do you call me good. There is none good but God."* What was Jesus saying? He was saying that you just called me good and there is none good but God as the bible states, so you just acknowledged that I was God. Then Jesus replied, *"What does the word of God say?"* The rich young ruler replied, *"To love God with all your heart, mind and soul, and to love your neighbor as yourself."* Jesus said, *"Well you have said."* The rich young ruler replied, *"I have done that from my youth. What lackest I?"* Jesus said, *"Sell everything that you own, give it to the poor and follow me."* The rich young ruler went away sad. What just happened here? This rich young ruler had an image of himself that was an ideal image. Unfortunately, it wasn't reality. He saw himself as loving god with his whole heart, mind and soul and his neighbor as himself and he thought he had been doing that from his youth. Jesus pointed out to him the reality and condition of his heart by giving him something to do. Basically, what Jesus was saying was, *"If that is true that you love God with your whole heart, mind and soul, and you just acknowledged that I was God by calling me good and by realizing that I have the ability to give eternal life, and you truly love your neighbor as yourself, then you will be able to sell everything you have and give it to the poor."* This would prove that you love your neighbor as yourself. The second command Jesus gave him showed that he didn't love God with his whole heart, mind and soul, because if he did, he would be able to follow Jesus and give up everything for him. Jesus confronted this man's ideal self with the real self because Jesus knew the condition of the man's heart and ours as well.

When you try to show or tell the person who is using the toxic behavior of being the abuser, that person will complain that you are trying to tell them what they should feel. It is not that you are trying to tell them what they feel; it's just that you are just pointing up the discrepancies between their image of themselves and reality. It goes like this....... *"Well if that is true, then do this or that...."* and if they can't seem to do it and it ruins their ideal image they had of themselves and the abuser goes away mad and sad like the rich young ruler, only they blame you and say that you are trying to tell them how they feel instead of taking a look at reality.

Let's take a look at it this way, if you went to a counselor you will have that counselor approaching your counseling sessions as if you are the one trying to tell the toxic abuser how they feel, because this is how the toxic abuser views this when you do this. It is the same thing Jesus did in order to bring the person to face reality, their sin and their condition in order to accept Jesus.

Now the whole counseling session is getting off track because the counselor thinks you're the one telling the toxic abuser how they feel, and you are the one who is controlling and the counselor has been conned. It is not that. You are just not buying the phony, false image that toxic abuser has of themselves. You will see what they do and how it doesn't line up with what he says. As in the scripture states; that you will know them by their fruits (Matthew 7:17-20 NIV, **"Likewise every good tree bears good fruit, but a bad tree bears bad fruit. A good tree cannot bear bad fruit, and a bad tree cannot bear good fruit. Every tree that does not bear good fruit is cut down and thrown into the fire. Thus, by their fruit you will recognize them."**).

You then are going to hold up the mirror to them in love every time and you are not going to allow them to stay in their deception and believe that they are something that they are not. If you will read your bible, you will see where Jesus did this repeatedly to people who thought more of themselves then they ought. (Romans 12:3 states, *"For by the grace given me I say to every one of you: Do not think of yourself more highly than you ought, but rather think of yourself with sober judgment, in accordance with the measure of faith God has given you."*)

Bottom line: The ideal self is the one we wish to be and the real self is the one we truly are. The real self is not ideal. Some people value the ideal self more than the real. The problem with the ideal self is that it is a fantasy and people who believe the fantasy are people who are deceived and they need other people from the outside to point out the discrepancies in what they believe and what they do

(Excerpts from Changes That Heal by Dr. Henry Cloud)

"The inherent problem in the relationship between the ideal and the real is that the ideal judges the real as unacceptable and brings down condemnation and wrath on the real (and anyone who points out the real). This sets up an adversarial relationship between the two, and like all adversaries, they move further and further apart. The further apart the real is from the ideal, the greater the deception and the more the person lives in a fantasy.

An important aspect of the relationship between the ideal and the real is its emotional tone. If we adopt a judgmental tone, one of condemnation and wrath toward what is real, then we have a divided house. Our ideals will judge and condemn our real self into nonexistence. We will use shame, guilt, hiding, denial, splitting, and other defenses to hide the real self. Whatever we do not accept in grace will be under judgment and condemnation, and we will hide it behind a psychological fig leaf".

Bottom line: Where there is defending, denial, blaming, minimizing, rationalizing, explaining, etc. there is deception. If a person does this continually, there is a major problem and that person lives in a fantasy world, not one of reality. This is a person that loves darkness rather than light and will not come to the light so that their deeds can be reproved, that they were wrought in darkness. This is where condemnation comes from. These are the people who are condemned and hell bound. This is a serious thing! This is a person who will betray his closest family members to protect himself and his own best interests. This is a person who calls evil, good and says that there is nothing wrong with what he did because.........etc, etc, etc!

This is a person who will never admit that he has a problem, that he lives in a phony, fantasy world, yet he has the nerve to tells others that his family members are **"unstable or mental"** when they, themselves, doesn't have a grip on reality.

~Repentance/Confession vs. Denial/ Defending~

A condition that needs to be met in order for a person to be saved and forgiven their sins is one of repentance and confession. The word "repent" means to change your mind about what you are doing and see it as God sees it and call it sin and go God's way and turn back toward God. Denial is the opposite of repentance. Denial and defending keep you from changing your mind about your behavior and it keep you in your sin and darkness. It blocks you from receiving any grace, forgiveness and reconciliation, both from God and the person you are in a relationship with. So to say, that manipulator, the abuser, that toxic person can be saved from this type of spirit.

Let's get deep in the scripture now; Judas was a manipulator and controller, not to mention a thief. Judas was a zealot. The zealots were rebel groups of people who wanted to overthrow the Roman rule over the Jews. The Jews believed that the Messiah would overthrow the Roman rule and return the kingdom to Israel and the Messiah would rule and reign from there. The disciples believed that Jesus would do this as well. One reason Judas joined Jesus as one of the disciples was because of this belief. When Jesus wasn't doing things the way

Judas thought they should be done, and then Judas thought he could force or manipulate the situation for everyone's good and best interest. You see, Judas was well intentioned. Jesus wasn't just taking over and ruling and reining the kingdom and overthrowing the Roman Empire as he wanted and thought he would. Judas thought that if he could force Jesus' hand and get them to take Him into captivity and force a confrontation between Jesus and the rulers, Jesus would have to fight then, and surely, being the Messiah, he would win and overthrow the Roman Empire and the oppression of the Jews would end as the scriptures had promised. Judas thought he was helping God fulfill the scriptures differently than the way he really ended up helping God fulfill the scriptures. He thought he would help God move in and obtain His rule and reign over Israel and set up His kingdom while overthrowing the Roman oppressors.

Well intentioned Judas didn't think that Jesus was doing things the way that he should. Judas thought he knew best how and when things should be done, so he tried to control and manipulate the situation to get what he thought would be best for himself, the Jews and the everyone concerned. In taking matters into his own hands because he thought he knew what was best and Jesus wasn't doing what he thought Jesus should, he tried to force Jesus into a situation that would cause Him to fight and set up His kingdom in Israel, thus freeing the Jews, and in the meantime, earn a little pocket money in the process. He thought he knew what was best. When Jesus was being crucified, and it didn't go down like Judas planned, then poor, deceived Judas went and hung himself. The bible says that Satan was behind all this and it was Satan who had entered Judas. Just because a person is well intentioned, doesn't mean that Satan won't use that.

Satan is behind all deception and darkness, manipulation and control. Manipulative, controlling people, even though well-intentioned, will betray you and God Himself. (Read more on Judas in Matthew 26:47-50)

What are the effects of living with someone who will not accept responsibility for his toxic behavior and keeps making excuses for it? It leaves his family with hopelessness and despair and feeling that things will never change. It leads to repressed anger and emotions that turn to depression, addictions and suicide in family members that lives with an abusive controller. It hurts and affects them physically, emotionally, spiritually and psychologically. It ruins and affects the victim's relationship with God because they feel abandoned by God and His people. You then have "so called Christians" turn their back on you or make things worse by telling you that God will not permit you to divorce this man, or that if the wife would just obey and submit, there wouldn't be a problem. God forbid!

Jesus never placed the rule above the needs of the people. That is why he was persecuted by the legalistic, law worshipping religious people. These people kept the letter of the law and missed the spirit of it. I had someone tell me that God would not permit me to divorce my ex because "God hates divorce". When I read the scripture in Malachi 2:16 which states; that God hates divorce, it is talking about domestic abuse. God is rebuking the church leaders and the men for the way they oppressed their spouses and because they dealt with their spouses treacherously. God was speaking to the husbands, wives, religious leaders and calling them to accountability. God said that he hated the violence done to the spouses and the fact that they covered the violence with their garments, and that they went to worship the Lord like everything was great and wonderful and they thought their relationship with God was great and wonderful. God was severely angry because these people were oppressing, controlling and abusing their spouses and going into the house of the Lord like nothing was wrong. Then the Lord calls these people to repentance, and he finishes it off by saying "I hate divorce". What was God's point in saying that he hated divorce?

I believe what God was saying in my opinion was that He hated the consequence of the sin of abusing, oppressing, and controlling of the spouses. The abusive spouse would come into the house of the Lord to worship like nothing was wrong, and nobody was doing anything about it and calling these people into accountability. The consequence of abusing your spouse, controlling and oppressing her/him is divorce and God permits and prefers divorce over what you are doing. Divorce, in this situation, is the consequence and provision permitted by God for the safety and protection of the woman and children. Divorce hurts and God hates it, but God permits it and allows it because God hates violence, oppression, abuse, and acting like nothing is wrong with it when coming into the house of the Lord to worship even more, so the Lord was calling them to repentance so that they would not have to go through the consequence of divorce or suffer God's judgment. Some pastors not all, quote the verse about God hating divorce in order to control or keep people from divorcing and they miss the whole point that God was trying to make.

More people need to read their bibles asking themselves this question, "What is God's point"? I'll give you a scripture verse and show you several ways people can read it.

People were questioning Jesus about divorce (Matthew 19:3). The Jewish people were divorcing their wives for every cause. If the woman didn't make the man's breakfast just right, she was given a write of divorcement and put out on the street with absolutely nothing. She could not remarry, get a job or anything. To a woman, this was equivalent to a death sentence and many women did die as a result. That was why the Jewish women started to take the dowry money and make it a part of their wedding veil or headpiece. That way if the man put them out or divorced them for any cause, they had their veil and the money in it to live off of. God permitted divorce through Moses. It was because of the hardness of the men's hearts. The divorce procedure that Moses put together said that the woman were allowed to remarry and that if the man was going to divorce them, he had to provide them with a home and everything they need. They were free to work, remarry and go about their life again. This was the provision God permitted through Moses because of the hardness of the men's hearts. It was not God's perfect will, but it was His permissive will. Billy Graham states that alimony or spousal support is the price a man pays for dealing with his wife treacherously. Now please don't get me wrong I am not telling you to go out now and get a divorce please do not misinterpret. What I am trying to tell you is that make sure you have exhausted all avenues first—counseling, prayer, more prayer and communication with your spouse.

(I don't know why God is dealing with me heavily in writing about this but thank God that he delivered me from bondage of divorce.) Now back to Jesus, there were two schools of thought in Jesus' day. One said that a man could put away (divorce) his wife for any cause. Another said that he could only divorce his wife for adultery. They asked Jesus which it was. Jesus replied that a man cannot put away his wife, except for fornication or adultery. Then he went on to say that if a man marries a woman who has been divorced, then he is guilty of adultery as well. What was Jesus' point? The point Jesus was trying to make was that most of the Jewish society was like our society today. Just about everybody is or has been divorced and remarried and therefore guilty of adultery. It was a major problem in their society just as it is today. What Jesus was trying to get them to see was that they were all in sin and in need of a savior and they were no different than anyone else! They were trying to justify their sin or divorce and trap Jesus in His words. He was trying to bring them to salvation by posing their sin AS GOD SEES IT.

Now a toxic abuser would have used this scripture to blame their spouse for the problems in their marriage. They would have said that they had all this trouble because they married a divorced woman or some excuse. That way they didn't have to look at themselves or their behavior. They had something else to blame it on. They forgot the scripture verse that says if a man marries a woman who has been divorced, he is guilty of adultery as well.

~Adultery is not just an act~

A legalistic person would read and hear that scripture as: *"Whatever you do, don't marry a divorced person or you are guilty of adultery."* For those people, Jesus goes on to say, ***"And if you even look at a woman and lust, you have an adulterous heart."*** Adultery is not just an act, it is a heart condition. Just because you don't perform the act, doesn't mean your heart isn't adulterous. Jesus pretty much posed the heart conditions of those who thought more of themselves then they ought because they kept the rule. He showed them that none of them were free of adultery or an adulterous heart in order to bring them to repentance because they could not or would not see their sin or heart condition, and they all had the same heart condition, which many self righteous people refused to look at or accept.

Read your bible by asking yourself, "What is the point"?

Because of the acts of abuser and the spouse not getting help their own children will have problem dealing with reality because of the abuse they witnessed in the home. They choose to be blissfully ignorant of things in life, pretending things are fine, when everything points to the fact that they are not. For example, my children were so shocked at the divorce. They loved both of us but didn't know who to trust because of the hurt they felt. They thought it was something they did to cause their father and me to divorce. Of course they were young and didn't understand fully. A lot of things I kept hidden from them to protect them. I didn't want my children to hate either of us especially for our wrong doing. Lesson learned you have to be open and communicate with your children about what is going on. If not it would be more devastating when they learn the truth! Ouch! Boy did I learn the hard way!!

Using Children

Making your spouse feel guilty about the children, using the children to relay messages, using visitation to harass your spouse, threatening to take the children away, brain washing the adult children and denying that abuse ever took place.

Most of this consists of how a toxic controlling abuser continues to victimize the woman or man after separation or divorce.

I must admit this but I am sure many of you reading this went through some of the things I written thus far in this book because boy I sure did! My ex used to control me by making me feel guilty about the kids. Even though I was in the military he didn't want me to reenlist simply because it was horrible for the kids. He wanted me home and cooking his meals 3 times a day. So of course being the "submissive lost wife" I did and grew tired and weary all the time! Now don't get me wrong there isn't anything wrong cooking for your spouse and/or tending to the children while he is at work IF you both choose to do this as a collective decision! But for me I was told and hinted by him that I needed to be at home and if I work I would be considered as a terrible, selfish mother. Anything else he didn't want me to do because he was insecure, he would come up with some excuse as to why it was bad for the kids and why I shouldn't do it. I couldn't even hang out with out with the wives because he was afraid I would talk about what was going on in our relationship. His words were *"this is our home and it is no one business what is going on here... do you hear me!"*

I wasn't permitted to talk to my ex about my feelings, hurts or anger in front of the kids or let alone in private. He really wanted me to keep my feeling and mouth shut and this is his way of silencing me. He would laugh at my hysterically when I tried to get him to see what he was doing to me. He would do this all the time to get me upset and that trigged to tears for that it was a way for me shut me up. Yes he may have been tall in statue and small built in body but he never allowed that to stop him being abusive towards me

One day, I was depressed and just wanted to be left alone. The last thing I wanted was to talk to him because he would just shame me for my feelings. I tried to avoid him. All I wanted to do was to be left alone to think and pray. I have learned being with him not to open my mouth if you don't want to get hurt or verbally abused. My ex saw how depressed I was and he kept following me around house asking me what was wrong as though he didn't know—mind games! I kept setting a boundary by asking him to leave me alone. This is one of the traits an abuser will do if they don't know what you are thinking, especially when he can't control your way of thinking. He can't fix it, so he gets real afraid and upset if you don't talk, so he follows you around and badgers you in order to get you to spill the beans or make you feel guilty because you don't talk. A loving person will give you time to collect your thoughts and asked "if there is something that we can pray about?" or "How can I fix this situation to make it better for you?"

The more I insisted that he just leave me alone and let me think and pray, the more insistent he got that I talk. Finally, he gets all upset and starts saying how silly I was. He says things in front of the kids to make me out as the bad person simply because I just wanted to be left alone. He will slam things or go in the bedroom slam closet doors. Just to let the kids see he is upset with me! They didn't know what was going on but they did see the anguish in his eyes and the tears flowing from my eyes. He got the kids all upset and afraid because he is all upset and afraid, because that is what he is thinking and he needed to control the situation.

He starts getting everyone all upset because he was telling everyone that I was going to leave him and make a big mess in the house and he was going to take the kids and leave that night so that they wouldn't be harmed by seeing me. And this man says that I am the one who harms my children. He doesn't see his behavior as harmful or cruel to anyone, because he is trying to protect and help. He is oblivious to the effects that this had on everyone that night. This ended in physical violence as well.

A paranoid schizophrenic does this kind of stuff *(now I am not calling my ex schizophrenic)*. They have a fear and that fear takes on a life of itself and they follow that fear in their mind to its logical conclusion, and they try to take control of a situation that doesn't even exist, but in their mind it is real. What do you think that does to children to be told that their mother is going to leave them by their father! How sick is that! I was just tired of arguing and debating. I was tired of being used and abused. I was tired of being controlled. I was tired of being the one who was someone stepping stool. I was tired of being a punching bag whether it was verbal, mental or physical abuse.

A toxic abuser is afraid.

A toxic abuser is afraid of their own emotions and other people's emotions if they are negative. They believe that some emotions are bad and you are a bad person if you have a "bad" or negative emotion. They think that if you feel something, then you will act upon it. That is the way the abuser is - controlled by his emotions. They think everyone else is the same way. A person can be depressed, sad or angry and not choose to do anything about it. Some people are comfortable with their emotions and accept them and don't label them as right or wrong, because they are not. It doesn't mean that you have to act upon them, though.

Now that we have divorced over some years ago, he has tried to brain washed my children into thinking that abuse never took place. They do not understand that abuse is a dynamic of control and manipulation. Any physical abuse that happened in our home never happened in front of the kids, it was more verbal and emotional abuse that happened in front of them and because of that, they now believe that I have lied about it, even though I have everything documented as proof, in the event anything is needed. The physical abuse happened at a time when they were very young and they didn't understand what was going on.

My children were in denial and believe their father who lied about me to isolate me from my children and gain support for him. For years I shielded my children from the abuse because I knew they love their father and especially since they were girls it would have been detrimental to them so I thought.

Years have trespassed and I had the opportunity to work overseas. While I was overseas working it was hard on me trying to deal with him using the children against me in not speaking to them telephonically. I ended up giving him the custody to take care of the children since I was stationed and couldn't bring them over. He would control the conversation simply because he wanted money from me which at first I thought was understandable but there was a hidden agenda. At first we had a communicable relationship because of the children and we had an agreement of the type of finances I will give the children. But he wanted the money to be given to him and not to the children.

This was another example of the type of controlling and manipulative spirit taken place after being divorced. He ended up getting married and his wife tag team against me. It gotten so bad where there were times I had to call the police to do a health and welfare check to make sure my children was okay. He was so needy when it comes to people liking him and thinking the best of him, and just like I used to be brainwashed by him. I kept thinking to myself during this testing period that God will vindicate me! I have just that kind of crazy faith in Him to believe that He will do that for me!

So for two years working overseas the ex would have private sessions talking about me to our children along with his wife in a negative way and he thought this was a way of punishing me, isolating me and using the kids. I was told by him and his wife that I would never see my children again and they will never ever have their mother in their life? Who does that? I mean he was married to a woman who had three children of her own so why in the world any women turn another mother against her children? Only someone who feel threaten to gain control of someone whom they can no longer control!! How very sad for the children who were caught in the cross fire and blinded. (As I once was). Although I don't blame them but I sure was upset during the whole ordeal. Yes my children love their daddy and yes they were in a place where they thought the environment was conducive. I was so angry with my children at first because when trying to explain to them what was **"REALLY"** going on they kept a brick wall up in defense to him and lashed out verbally towards me!! I just gave up and learned *that they don't get it because they don't want to right now!* It is less painful for them to believe the lies than to believe the things that actually took place in the 12 years their parents were married. Again I do not blame them because they were young and not understanding what truly was going on.

How many know that you are no longer condemned for actions that are no longer your fault. In Romans 8:1 states, ***"There is therefore now no condemnation to them which are in Christ Jesus, who walk not after the flesh, but after the Spirit."***

How abusive and sad it is to use children of any age to punish a spouse. I believe this is sick and this is the reason that some states make parents take classes on what a divorce does to children, especially when they are used as weapons to punish the spouse. It is the kids that loose. I have kept all the calls and emails that I have just in case when the kids want to know the truth and when they want to stop being used and manipulated. Maybe someday they will realize that it must have been pretty bad for their mother to be so depressed that she would rather drown than live another day married to their father. (Thank goodness for deliverance in that area. It was hard but I made it over!!)

It must not have been "made up lies" if their mother was in hospital so many times with sickness and depression that was off the charts. They have been convinced by their father that I have made it all up and I believe that they won't look at any of the documentation. Unfortunately, my kids at the time never cared about my pain or my feelings simply because of what they were experiencing. They didn't understand what was really going on and for what was displayed was their parents were divorced and battling.

I recall a time years later when I had visitation rights to see my children simply because I was stationed overseas Kuwait where at the time we agreed that he will have them and I will see them for vacations. I followed everything my lawyer told me to do and that was to notify him before April 1st (in which

I notified him by email, letter, text and phone call on December year prior and every month until my visitation) and it was confirmed by him that it was okay. On my way to get my daughters I called him and told him I was on my way but in quick conversation his first question was "why I wouldn't pay him extra $1000?" What he didn't quite understand was I sent close to $2000 to him in the children name for child support that month so why would I give him more money?? He not only had our three daughters but NOW wife has 3 children so I wasn't about to financially take care of them!! So what he do in retaliation and manipulating--he yelled out of the front door of his home as my daughters was about to come out of the house to get in my car—to get back in the house you are NOT going to be with your Mother!! Now who does that?? A person who claims that he is a "man of God" decides to manipulate the situation and avoid the children in spending time with the mother of his children?? Really!!!! Lord Jesus helped me that day because in my flesh I wanted to break that door down and him too! But God!! After battling back and forth for two more years with this man in seeing my children; spending time and calling my children. God came through for me where he had to pay back child support, I regained custody of my children and my sanity was intact—Praise JESUS!

My feelings were always openly negated in front of my children. I was always treated disrespectfully in front of the kids from my ex as they grew up, so they never respected me as well for that toxic spirit was rooted in them. With that being done for so long my daughters always felt and acted like they were my equal. This came up in counseling several times when I went after my divorce. I told the counselor that my children were only concerned with themselves, their feelings and what they wanted or needed. I have always been invisible to everyone most of my life, even my parents and siblings. Rationalize my feelings and pain away and they don't exist in their eyes. My parents and the ex have never cared about me or how I might be feeling or how much I might be hurting. Again thank you Lord for keeping me but I wouldn't change a thing or go back to change the past. This was definitely a lesson learned in a HARD WAY!!

But what really hit home when my husband Jay said "ENOUGH IS ENOUGH! NO ONE IS GOING TO DO THIS TO MY WIFE-- THE DEVIL IS A LIAR!" Seeing the pain in my husband eyes of all the attacks I was going through I didn't realize how it was hurting him as well!

I know you all are saying *"Oh wow Marshell you went through so much!"* Or some of you may be saying *"Why did you stay so long?"* or *"Why didn't you just leave!"* Again if you read my first book "Broken to Forgive When other's Don't!" you will understand why. It was hard on me and I wasn't as strong as I am today. God wasn't in my life back then like he is now. I wasn't strong in relying on Him to take care of my problems or knew that he was my source and protector. I had to be broken—God knew and understood!

Even still did well towards my parents, I love them despite how they treat me especially since the relationship was broken. I wanted my children to spend time and develop a relationship with them but I knew my limits so I still told my children to see their grandparents when it was allowed. They were allowed to call them, write and I even paid for my daughter and her fiancé (who is now her husband) to travel to see them. My prayer for my daughters; now, that they will learn the lessons that were presented before them that when they have children of their own they won't use the same toxic behavior and abusive techniques. I do not want the sins of the forefathers be visited upon my children (Exodus 20:5). My thoughts when I was divorced, *"Oh God how I wish I had gotten out years before when they were young. Oh God, how I wish I had the support years ago to have gotten out of the marriage so that these dynamics were not passed down to my kids, who will do them and pass them down to theirs.* I pled the blood of Jesus over their lives daily!"

Using Male Dominance

Treating her like a servant, making all the big decisions, acting like the "master of the castle", being the one to define men's and women's roles.

Putting you above her and treating her like a child. This is the way an abuser would treat you. If you said that you were going to do something and the abuser didn't disapprove, they would say, "That is all right with me". It was like you needed their approval, permission or something in order to do things. You would say to them, "I don't need your permission".

Another scenario: Whenever you give your input to small or large decisions in the relationship, if they were not the same view he/she had, your opinion, feelings, wants, needs or view was explained away or negated. If you persisted, you then got shamed or put down. How many of you all reading this can say this happened to you? Well for me I learned to keep my mouth shut if the thing was not that important to me because it was not worth the pain and shame inflicted on me in order to press my opinion or wants or to get what I wanted. I rarely got what I wanted because the toxic abuser thought they knew what was best for everyone and if you weren't in agreement with them, you were going to be hurt verbally if you expressed a different view. It was their way or no way!!

Example: The ex had his superior male role thing and everyone else was subject to him and beneath him and that is how he treated all of us, as less than or not as good as. The kids had no respect for me because the spouse didn't. They started to treat me as their equal and as one of their playground buddies. They wouldn't listen to anything I said because their father didn't. He disrespected me in front of the kids on a continual basis, all in the name of what is best for the family. How do you expect the kids to respect the mother and obey her if the father doesn't listen to her and shows no respect for her and he is in control and runs things? This translated to even the smallest of things in the household. He was the master of the home and he decided what went in the house. As you can guess, this became a major issue and this was about the time I started sticking up for myself.

Using Economic Abuse

Preventing her from getting or keeping a job, making her ask for money, giving her an allowance, taking her money, not letting her know about or have access to family income.

Abusive, controlling people are fearful people where money is concerned. They are so tight with money they squeak and they are constantly sending a message to their family that their money is more important than you and your needs.

When the ex and I got married, I had excellent credit. Although I didn't know how to handle money so for that the ex used that as his opportunity (*at the time I didn't know he didn't have good credit—man I wish the lighten bolt hit me in the head!)* I had to ask the ex for money for everything, like a child has to ask his father. I didn't have access to the checkbook to get groceries or anything I had to ask permission. I had credit cards but it was maxed out or wanted me to buy to excess the limits that cause my credit to damage. No matter how much money we had in the savings account, I was made to feel guilty about buying things for the kids, myself or the home. It got so bad that I couldn't buy anything without suffering from extreme guilt. That is how pathetic it had gotten and that is when I realized there was a major problem going on here. It didn't matter if we had $15,000 in the savings account at the time. I was not allowed to work after leaving the military (until about 5 years later in the marriage). But when he told me that it was okay to work (because we were struggling financially) I took this has a "good thing!" That was the only way I could safely enter the work force without suffering verbal abuse. I was glad to work and that is how I felt when I was living in my parents' house in my teenage years.

Later in the years of marriage everything was getting tensed and were weren't spending time as husband and wife. Things transpired and sin settled in the home! I was so lost spiritually, mentally and emotionally where I didn't know where I was coming or going! I back slide in the world and did what the world did. I didn't care anymore of my marriage with the ex because he simply didn't care about me with what he was doing!! But the abuse intensified where the ex would try to get me fired by showing up at my place of employment all the time and whenever a male would enter the room, the ex would put his hands all over me, like he was marking his territory just as a dog would. I definitely felt like a piece of property and it was extremely inappropriate. He had me followed!!

The list goes on and on but it would take all day what he did but I let go and LET GOD!! I learned that no matter you cannot change anyone who doesn't want to be changed. Only God can do that. He had his reasoning and rational as to why he did what he did. I use to question and wondered *"Do real Christians do this?"* Did I truly marry a sheep in wolves clothing. Sigh! Anyway, economic abuse is an abusive technique used by domestic abusers to control their victim. He tries to control and hold on to this right to the very end! He'll swear up and down that he is not an abuser. Thank God for my gift that I have NOW. My angel Jonathan-Jay Forte! Whew-- where had he been all my life!

Using Coercion and Threats

Making and/or carrying out threats to do something to hurt her, threatening to leave her, divorce her, to commit suicide, to report her to welfare, making her drop charges, making her do illegal things.

Oh, here is a good example. I overheard someone saying that their spouse threatened to divorce them if they go to someone outside the family for help and acknowledgment or if they tell anyone that what he does that is controlling or abusive. He wants them to shut up and he doesn't want anyone to know what he does and what he is like. They had to keep up this image of "the perfect family". How many know there isn't a thing as a "Huxtuble family?!"

It's even hard to say right now that I've been verbally and mentally abused for saying anything to someone outside the family and what I have said is true, but if he goes and tells people things about me, that is okay? It is okay for him to tell people that I was mental, unstable, adulterous or unfaithful, but if I tell pastors or people of the abusive, controlling things he has done, I get abused and threatened. Isn't that crazy--what an oxymoron? I remember a time when I filed charges against him he coerced me to drop an order of protection against him saying I will not be financial stable to take care of the children if I had him kicked out of the military. Even though I knew he didn't have a leg to stand on but YES I wasn't financial stable because I didn't have a job at the time I felt trapped and he knew I needed him.

The thing is, they threaten you with this type of manipulation in order to control you and get you to drop charges or orders of protection. They feel betrayed if you go outside the family to get help, but they do not feel they are betraying you when they tell others that you are unstable, mental, adulterous or unfaithful in order to discredit you and isolate you from anyone that would help or support you. That is toxic control!

You will notice that physical violence is not listed on the power and control wheel. Toxic abuse is about power and control and it doesn't always mean or just mean physical abuse. A spouse usually resorts to physical violence when the other methods of controlling his or her family don't work anymore. A light bulb went off in my head years later after speaking to my friend Marry. She told me that The Lord said her as she was praying for me, *"Marshell, he only has as much control over you as you give him. So who really has the control"?* I looked at her with tears in my eyes and told her *"I do!"* Right then I was set free--I wasn't going to give in to the abuser anymore! I started setting boundaries. When the abuser could not control me anymore with all the things listed on the power and control abuse wheel, which is when physical violence resulted.

Abuse is about control and power! God does not want any spouse to submit to this abuse. We are to submit to God first and if the spouse wants you to do something that God does not, Jesus is your Lord first and foremost. Jesus said to think not that He came to bring peace, but a sword. Pray for them that they get in line with God.

This is what I have suffered with for 11 years not including the abuse I felt from my parents and this is why I was hurting and was depressed and isolated from people. I needed that healing power and needed to be delivered. Thank you Jesus for your deliverance and your healing power in my life! You stepped in when I was on my last leg about to tip over! You sent laborers who were praying for me and interceding on my behalf, who spoke life in my dead situation because you gave them a glimpse of my future! I give you praise Jesus!

Many Christians living for God have experienced the same thing and there is no shame in feeling that way. If you believe and live according to God's word and you will not compromise, then Satan is going to make your life hell and he will use the people closest to you to do it, too! Sad but true! Know this one thing that the God I know and worship validates and accepts your feelings. He doesn't negate them and he comes into your life to let you know that He knows how you feel and that you are not alone. There is a song by the Christian group called [8]"Virtue". The song is called "My Body" and God has used this song to minister to me, comfort me and validate my feelings as someone who has been abused. It is a song that the ladies are is singing about that your body is the Lord's temple and you are God's property. God saw his little girl who has suffered abuse at the hands of the abuser. Thank God for setting me free!

To be humble.

The word "humiliate" versus "to humble". I believe toxic abusers get this confused. It doesn't mean that you must humiliate to control an individual by being abusive to them. Submission in love according to the Word will get you what you need according to God statues and laws. Because the toxic abuser has such a fear of man and what others think of him, he wasn't worthy of Him, meaning Jesus, as the bible states. The abuser is like the tree planted, in the bible, where the owner came looking for fruit after many years. There wasn't any there. (In Matthew 7:19 NIV states, *"Every tree that does not bear good fruit is cut down and thrown into the fire."*) The gardener told the owner, "Let me dig around it and fertilize a little longer to see if it will produce anything". Years later, the returns and still no fruit and he say, "Dig it up. Don't let it burden the ground any further ". There can come a time when God cuts you off because you have wearied Him! You can miss the hour of your visitation and God will remove His protective covering from you and you will receive His judgment. The word "judgment" means "crisis" or the "time when it is decided when something shall live or die". The lack of fruit on you after Jesus, the Truth, has dug around you, watered you with the water of the word and fertilized you can be the determining factor of whether you will be judged. Passivity is not an option when God has brought Truth into your life to wash you in the water of the word in order to change you. As Jesus told Peter when He knelt to wash Peter's feet and Peter wouldn't let Him, *"If you don't allow Me to wash you, you have no part with Me"*! No part means no part, period. When God gives you the Truth, He expects you to act upon it and we are judged according to the Truth God has given us in our lives and what we have done with it. Be free from being the toxic abuser! Allow Jesus to change you so you can be NEW!

Before this book I wrote a book called, *"Broken to Forgive When others Don't"* thanking God for birthing that in me to forgive because it was hard. I wanted everyone to experience what I was feeling during that season in my life and I even told my ex to get the book as well so that healing can be brought about by his acknowledging what he has done and the immense pain that He has caused because he has spent so much time and energy denying it. I don't know if he purchased it but I only can pray that God will heal him totally from the inside out. I cannot worry if he is walking upright because only God can fix him and even though things are the way it is...he is still my brother in Christ and I must pray for him and let it go!

~Need Love versus Sacrificial Love~

Two types of Love C. S. Lewis said that there are two kinds of love. The first kind of love is NEED LOVE. Need love look good on the outside to the undiscerning?! They appear kind and considerate or the "nice person" to others. The difference is that they go out empty and do something for someone else so that they can feel good about themselves. They use others to meet their needs and get their self worth. This is an example of a Toxic abuser. These people look very responsible and considerate as they go about doing things for you. They do these things to get filled up and they are very concerned about how others view them and that you notice the things that they do. They are very self focused and self centered and they will suck the life out of you, just as a tare. The abuser has a reputation of: If you ask them what time it is, they will tell you how to make a clock. They love to talk about themselves and loves an audience. As the bible states, **"When words are many, sin is not absent, but he who holds his tongue is wise."** Proverbs 10:19 NIV

In other words, we are here admonished concerning the government of the tongue, that necessary duty of a Christian. 1. It is good to say little, because *in the multitude of words there wanteth not sin,* or *sin doth not cease.* Usually, those that speak much speak much amiss, and among many words there cannot but be many idle words, which they must shortly give an account of. Those that love to hear themselves talk do not consider what work they are making for repentance; for that will be wanted, and first or last will be had, where *there wanteth not sin.* 2. It is therefore good to *keep our mouth as with a bridle: He that refrains his lips,* that often checks himself, suppresses what he has thought, and holds in that which would transpire, is a wise man; it is an evidence of his wisdom, and he therein consults his own peace. Little said is soon amended, (Read also Amos 5:13 and James 1:19).

The second kind of love is SACRIFICIAL LOVE. This person goes out full and gives out of their own fullness at their own expense, expecting nothing in return. They use themselves to meet the other person's needs. They freely give what they have freely received from the Lord. They are the wheat that die to self to bring forth fruit in order to feed someone else. They are not concerned about how others view them or if their efforts get noticed. They say what they mean and mean what they say.

In Romans 5: 1-12; 21 states, *"Therefore being justified by faith, we have peace with God through our Lord Jesus Christ: By whom also we have access by faith into this grace wherein we stand, and rejoice in hope of the glory of God. And not only so, but we glory in tribulations also: knowing that tribulation worketh patience; And patience, experience; and experience, hope: And hope maketh not ashamed; because the love of God is shed abroad in our hearts by the Holy Ghost which is given unto us.*

For when we were yet without strength, in due time Christ died for the ungodly. For scarcely for a righteous man will one die: yet peradventure for a good man some would even dare to die. But God commendeth his love toward us, in that, while we were yet sinners, Christ died for us. Much more then, being now justified by his blood, we shall be saved from wrath through him. For if, when we were enemies, we were reconciled to God by the death of his Son, much more, being reconciled, we shall be saved by his life. And not only so, but we also joy in God through our Lord Jesus Christ, by whom we have now received the atonement. Wherefore, as by one man sin entered into the world, and death by sin; and so death passed upon all men, for that all have sinned: Verse [21] That as sin hath reigned unto death, even so might grace reign through righteousness unto eternal life by Jesus Christ our Lord."

Many people have copies of the 10 Commandments hanging on a wall. That's fine! But Jesus gave us a New Commandment.

 And you don't see it getting as much attention as the 10 Commandments. Jesus says in JOHN 13:34 states,

"A new commandment I give unto you, That ye love one another; as I have loved you, that ye also love one another."

To understand what Jesus commands us to do...we first have to understand how Jesus loves us. The word "love" in that verse is the Greek word AGAPE. It's a sacrificial type of love. It's a love that is so strong that a person will sacrifice his own interests... to meet the needs of another.

Jesus loves us so much...He was willing to give up the glories of Heaven come down here endure the agony and shame of the cross...so that you and I would have the opportunity to live with Him. That's Agape love!

~Love is a subject of Importance~

"Love" is one of the most common, yet misused and misunderstood words in the English language. On the bookshelf, "love" is synonymous with "romance" and seldom used without a sexual connotation. On television, love is depicted by programs like "Love Boat." Commercials tempt the audience to pay for a call to a "love connection," where companions can be matched or where romantic secrets are told.

Even Christians have a very fuzzy grasp of the meaning of love. The lyrics of all too many contemporary Christian songs use the word love in a way that falls far short of that which the Bible defines and describes. "I love the way you love me" are the words of one song. The meaning seems to be, "I love the warm, fuzzy way you treat me and make me feel so good." Toyota's television commercial says the same thing: *"I love whatcha do for me—Toyota."* No mention is made of God Himself, of who He is. There is no mention of the chastening of the Lord as a manifestation of His love for us (see Hebrews 12:3-13). There is no mention of our subordination or service, to God or to others.

Love is a subject of vital importance, not only because of our fuzzy ideas about what love really is, but because love is a matter of highest priority: ***"But now abide faith, hope, and love, these three; but the greatest of these is love"*** (1 Corinthians 13:13).

For a number of reasons, Paul regards love as greater even than faith and hope. To show the magnitude of the importance of our study, allow me to summarize these.

(1) Love is greater than faith and hope because love is eternal, while faith and hope is temporal (see 1 Corinthians 13:8-13). Because that which God has promised cannot presently be seen, faith and hope are necessary in this life. But when the perfect comes, when our Lord returns and we are living eternally in His presence, we will no longer need faith, for we shall see Him and experience all that He has promised. Our hope will be fulfilled. Our *love* for Him, however, will last for all eternity, inspiring our worship and service in His presence.

(2) *Love is the appropriate response to God's love and grace, in Christ* (see Luke 7:42, 47).

(3*) Love is the great commandment and one of the distinguishing marks of a true disciple of our Lord* (Matthew 22:37; Mark 12:33; Luke 6:27-36; John 13:35; 15:12-13).

(4) *Love facilitates and contributes to Christian unity* (John 17:20-26; Colossians 2:2; 3:14).

(5) *Love is the lubricant which greatly reduces the friction which can build up between us and others* (Ephesians 4:2; 1 Peter 4:8).

(6) Love is a key motive for our obedience to our Lord's commands (John 14:15, 21, 23, 24; 15:10; 21:15-17; 1 John 5:2; 2 John 1:16).

(7) Love is a stabilizing factor in our lives (Ephesians 3:17).

(8) Love is the goal of Paul's teaching as it should be the goal of all Christian teaching (1Timothy 1:5).

(9) Love is the one command which encompasses all aspects of our Christian life (Romans 13:8-10; 1 Corinthians 16:14).

(10) Love makes our service more profitable to others and to us (1 Corinthians 8:1; 13:1-13).

(11) Love is a key element in our defenses against Satan's attacks and devices (1Thessalonians 5:8).

*(12) **Our** love can and should be constantly growing* (Philippians 1:9; 1Thessalonians 3:12; 2 Thessalonians 1:3; Hebrews 10:24; 2 Peter 1:7).

(13) Our love can grow cold, especially in difficult times (Matthew 24:12; Revelation 2:4).

The vital role love must play in our Christian experience, and the very fuzzy concept of love prevalent today, makes our study one of great urgency and importance. We will search to learn what love is and how love behaves as described by Paul in our text.

The Context and Structure of Our Text

Paul focused our attention in chapters 1-11 on the "mercies of God" (see 12:1) which provide the basis and motivation for our Christian conduct. In chapters 12-15, Paul will describe the kind of behavior which the "grace" of God enables and expects. Verses 1 and 2 of chapter 12 are a general call to offer up our bodies as living sacrifices to God through a life of service. The exercise of our spiritual gifts is spoken of in verses 3-8 as one dimension of our sacrificial service. Now, in verses 9-21, Paul describes our sacrificial service as a walk in love. We are to demonstrate love toward the brethren (verses 9-13) and toward those outside the faith (verses 14-21). Right now let's focus on verses 9-13 and the necessity to walk in love in our relationships within the body of Christ. Paul will give us a working definition of what love is, and especially how love serves others, sacrificially, as unto the Lord.

In the internal structure of our text, I see verse 9 as the general, introductory statement and verses 10-13 as supporting descriptions of how love is manifested in various ways. Verse 10 describes Christian love as subordinating self-interest to give preference to the one loved. Verse 11 describes the energy and diligences which love stimulates, to carry through with those tasks which build up the other. Verse 12 points to the future hope which enables Christian love to endure present hardship and adversity. Verse 13 highlights two particular needs which love should be eager to meet: (1) the need for physical and financial help and (2) the need for hospitality.

A Preliminary Definition of Love

A preliminary definition of love will be helpful to prepare the way for this writing. The following is a composite definition based upon the teaching of the Scriptures as a whole.

Love is the heart-felt affection of the Christian in response to the love God has shown toward us, especially in the gift of salvation through our Lord Jesus Christ. Love is an affection which prompts the Christian to action. Love is first and foremost directed toward God and then toward others in an order of priority: God, family (especially our mate), fellow-believers, our neighbor, and even our enemy. Love subordinates the interests of the lover to the one who is loved. Love inspires our deliberate, diligent, self-sacrificial service to others, which is intended for their good, at our expense.

Love's Relationship to Righteousness (12:9)

Let love be without hypocrisy. Abhor what is evil; cling to what is good.

[11]Joseph Fletcher, an advocate of situational ethics, once told the story of a farmer whose daughter was seduced by a traveling salesman. Incensed by the violation of his sister, the girl's brother was ready to exterminate the salesman with his shotgun. Stepping in, the father admonished his son with the words: "Son, you are so full of what's right that you've lost sight of what's good."

Situational ethics is a term which is hardly used any more. This is not because the theory is passing, but because it is so widespread, no one thinks of it as something distinct. Our whole society is situational in its ethics. Situational ethics does not define morality and immorality in terms of biblical revelation, but in terms of "love." Moral judgment is determined by the existence or absence of love. A sexual union outside of marriage, but which is thought to be the expression of "love," is considered moral. The question then becomes, "Is it loving?" rather than, "Is it right?" If it is "loving," it is presumed to be right.

Not so with Paul's understanding of love. Biblical love cannot be separated from biblical righteousness. Christian love is drawn toward "right" and repulsed by "wrong." It is attracted to and adheres to that which is "good," abhorring and withdrawing from "evil." Christian love is most certainly not "blind." Biblical love distinguishes between good and evil, and then acts accordingly, cleaving to the good and avoiding the evil.

Christian love is something like a battery. There must be two poles for current to flow. There is a positive terminal and a negative terminal. In biblical thinking, "love" cannot be separated from "hate." Love is a choice, a decision. It is a decision to choose one thing and to reject another. Jacob could not "love" both Leah and Rachel; he had to "love" one and to "hate" the other.[53] So too we cannot serve two masters, for we will inevitably "love" one and "hate" the other (see Matthew 6:24).

Our love as Christians is to be both a *response* to God's love and a *reflection* of His love. Our Lord's love was a far cry from the hypocritical "love" of the scribes and Pharisees of His day. They spoke of good, but in practice they did what was evil. While our Lord's love prompted Him to receive sinners, and to suffer and to die for their salvation, it also manifested itself in Jesus' strong reaction to evil (see Matthew 20:12-17; 23:1-39). Jesus wanted no association with evil, and thus He even forbade the evil spirits to proclaim that He was the promised Messiah (see Mark 3:11-12).

There are Christians today who urge us to emphasize God's love. This we should do. But if we are to proclaim God's love, we must distinguish between good and evil. The love of God is that love which clings to the good and abhors the evil. The love of God cannot and does not overlook sin nor the judgment which it deserves and requires. If we would speak more of God's love, we must speak more of good and of evil. Rebuke and discipline are not a violation of love but a manifestation of it. Love acts in accordance with righteousness.

Love Subordinates "Self-Interest" to the Best Interest of Others (12:10)

Be devoted to one another in brotherly love; give preference to one another in honor.

Paul's words here speak of brotherly love; love expressed one to another, among Christians. Of all the "loves" mentioned in the New Testament, love for the brethren is one of the most prominent (see, for example, John 13:34-35; 15:12, 13, 17; Romans 13:8; 1 Peter 1:22; 2:17; 4:8; 1 John 2-4). This love marks us apart as disciples of our Lord (John 13:35; 15:12-13). This is the brotherly love in view in verse 10.

Love not only distinguishes between good and evil, it distinguishes between us and those we love. Christian love, according to Paul's words, produces a strong devotion among those who believe in Jesus Christ. Brotherly love gives preference to our brothers in Christ, placing them above us.

A disturbingly false view of love has become popular among Christians. This view holds that "self-love" is essential to, and the prerequisite of, love for others. This way of thinking insists that we cannot love God or others until we have first come to love ourselves. Self-love therefore becomes primary; the source of all other "loves." In Paul's mind, *this is pure hypocrisy.*

Christian love, by its very nature, subordinates the interests of the lover to those of the one loved. In Paul's own words, love is to "give preference to one another." This preference to others has its boundaries. *Preference*, according to Paul, *is to be given others in the realm of honor:* "give preference to one another <u>in honor</u>." "Self-esteem" is to be subordinated to "others-esteem."

As suggested, there are limits to what Paul is saying. Giving honor to others means that we seek the best interests of others, in love. But this does not mean that our love always takes the form that others may wish or even accept. Sometimes a brother or sister in Christ will expect—even demand—what is "evil" or what is detrimental to their spiritual growth. Sometimes a brother may wish to be affirmed or encouraged when he needs to be rebuked, in love. Love does not always give the other what he or she wants, but rather what is best. Often there is a higher price to pay when our love takes an unwelcome form.

Loving one another means serving others ahead of oneself but there are times when serving others means choosing not to serve, for the sake of stewardship and the sake of the gospel. Recognizing that I am but one member in the body of Christ and that God has gifted each member means I need not and cannot meet every need that I see. For me to meet a particular need may actually prevent someone else from doing so. Even when one member may do a better job, the gifts of others must be discovered and developed. This can only take place through experience in ministry.

Ministering to one individual could also hinder ministry to a larger number of people. Spending inordinate time with one individual may prevent one from devoting himself to a broader ministry. A true servant's spirit always is *willing* to help anyone at any time in the most menial task. Nevertheless, we must also maintain a strong sense of our own gifts and calling, exercising wisdom in our stewardship of that which God has given us to do.

So we see that love engenders the spirit of subordination, promoting servant hood and service one to another.

Love Handles Hardship by Focusing on Hope (12:12)

Rejoicing in hope, persevering in tribulation, devoted to prayer.

The staying power of love is closely related to its constant companions, faith and hope. Here Paul emphasizes love's endurance in the midst of adversity. The Christian life is not a warm fuzzy; it is a war. Love must be able to handle the hard times which are sure to come. Because we love God, the world will hate us. We will find that living in a fallen world brings about suffering and groaning. Paul has spoken of this in chapters 5 and 8. Interestingly, love is prominent in these two chapters as well. The love prominent in chapters 5 and 8 is the love of God for us. Now, in our text, Paul turns to our love and its endurance in times of tribulation and testing.

Perseverance in tribulation is accomplished by rejoicing in hope. Paul speaks of the role of hope in a general way but also in the form of a personal testimony:

And not only this, but we also exult in our tribulation, knowing that tribulation brings about perseverance; and perseverance, proven character; and proven character, hope; and hope does not disappoint, because the love of God has been poured out within our hearts through the Holy Spirit who was given to us (Romans 5:3-5).

Therefore we do not lose heart, but though our outer man is decaying, yet our inner man is being renewed day by day. For momentary, light affliction is producing for us an eternal weight of glory far beyond all comparison, while we look not at the things which are seen, but at the things which are not seen; for the things which are seen are temporal, but the things which are not seen are eternal (2 Corinthians 4:16-18).

What contrast there is between Christian love and the "love" of this world? The heathen mind reasons, "Eat, drink, and be merry, for tomorrow we die" (1 Corinthians 15:32; see also Luke 12:19 and 1 Corinthians 10:7). Believing there is no future, the unbeliever must strive to wring out of the present all of the pleasure he can. The Christian is just the opposite:

By faith Moses, when he had grown up, refused to be called the son of Pharaoh's daughter; choosing rather to endure ill-treatment with the people of God, than to enjoy the passing pleasures of sin; considering the reproach of Christ greater riches than the treasures of Egypt; for he was looking to the reward (Hebrews 11:24-26).

The suffering saint may be tempted to think God is far from him in his times of adversity. This is not the case. God is never more near us than in our trials. It is in our sufferings that we find a deeper fellowship with Christ than we would have otherwise known:

Let your way of life be free from the love of money, being content with what you have; for He Himself has said, *"I WILL NEVER DESERT YOU, NOR WILL I EVER FORSAKE YOU," so that we confidently say, "The LORD IS MY HELPER, I WILL NOT BE AFRAID. WHAT SHALL MAN DO TO ME?"* (Hebrews 13:5-6).

Therefore, since Christ has suffered in the flesh, arm yourselves also with the same purpose, because he who has suffered in the flesh has ceased from sin (1 Peter 4:1).

Beloved, do not be surprised at the fiery ordeal among you, which comes upon you for your testing, as though some strange thing were happening to you; but to the degree that you share the sufferings of Christ, keep on rejoicing; so that also at the revelation of His glory, you may rejoice with exultation. If you are reviled for the name of Christ, you are blessed, because the Spirit of glory and of God rests upon you (1 Peter 4:12-14).

Love Puts Privacy in Its Place (12:13)

Contributing to the needs of the saints, practicing hospitality.

When times get tough, people begin to tighten up and to take fewer risks. Jesus warned His disciples that the love of the saints would wane in the days of tribulation:

And Jesus answered and said to them, *"See to it that no one misleads you. For many will come in My name, saying, 'I am the Christ,' and will mislead many. And you will be hearing of wars and rumors of wars; see that you are not frightened, for those things must take place, but that is not yet the end. For nation will rise against nation, and kingdom against kingdom, and in various places there will be famines and earthquakes. But all these things are merely the beginning of birth pangs. Then they will deliver you up to tribulation, and will kill you, and you will be hated by all nations on account of My name. At that time many will fall away and will betray one another and hate one another. Many false prophets will arise, and will mislead many simply because lawlessness is increased, most people's love will grow cold. But the one who endures to the end, it is he who shall be saved. And this gospel of the kingdom shall be preached in the whole world for a witness to all the nations, and then the end shall come"* (Matthew 24:4-14).

False teachers will appear, Jesus warned, leading many astray (verses 5, 11). Wars, earthquakes, and famines will increase, creating racial and national tensions and multiplying physical needs (verse 7). This will be only the beginning of trouble (verse 8). Christians will be the special focus of hate and opposition (verse 9). Many saints will fall away, denying their faith (verse 10). Lawlessness will also increase. Anarchy will prevail. In such times, the love of most will grow cold and sometimes turn to hate (verses 10, 12).

In hard times, love toward the brethren will be needed more than ever. By this love, others will know we are Christians. At the same time, showing love will be more risky and dangerous than ever. Such times seem to be coming upon the church in America today, as they have come upon the church elsewhere. As such times come upon us, the need for love of the brethren increases.

Paul calls for two particular expressions of love for the brethren in verse 13. Both expressions invade the privacy of the Christian, a privacy highly valued in a self-centered, self-indulgent society. These two expressions of brotherly love involve first the wallet and second the home. Paul exhorts Christians to "contribute to the needs of the saints" and to aggressively practice hospitality. Let us consider both of these expressions of brotherly love.

I believe Christians have, in many instances, rightly perceived the threat to their families coming from our heathen culture. We are not far behind Sodom and Gomorrah, if indeed we are behind at all! But there is a danger that our homes can become fortresses from which we bar not only our enemies but strangers who profess to know Christ. *Practicing hospitality is vital to practicing our love for the brethren.* When danger increases, along with the risk factor, love for the brethren becomes an even greater matter of urgency. When the risks increase, our love becomes an even greater matter of faith and hope.

Even when there is no great threat, as there was in the days of Sodom and Gomorrah, there are still reasons why Christians hole up in their homes, refusing to show hospitality by inviting others into their homes. It is an invasion of our privacy as suggested. But it also exposes us as we really are, especially any hypocrisy we sustain by keeping others at arm's length. It is an invasion into the intimacy of the home, an intimacy which we should share but would rather not. It allows us to look closer at the needs of the stranger, so that we may discover other needs and thus other obligations to which we must respond. Paul's exhortation is clear. *Hospitality is our obligation. It is one of the manifestations of the Christian's "love for the brethren."*

One word of clarification should be made here. We are told to be **"wise as serpents and harmless as doves"** (Matthew 10:16). We ought not to be naive or foolish as to where we stay nor to whom we invite into our homes. The hospitality which Paul calls for here is hospitality to the brethren. We are not encouraged to invite anyone and everyone into our homes. We should not hesitate to inquire as to the testimony of those whom we bring into our homes, especially if they are invited for more than just a meal. And even those who are saints should be shown hospitality in such a way as to minimize needless, foolish risks.

The song with the words, "What the world needs now is love, sweet love" is true. The world does need love. It needs the love of God. That love has been poured out in the person of Jesus Christ. Before you can ever be an instrument of God's love, you must first be a recipient of that love.

The love of God is not the kind of love men naturally desire. That is because God's love is a righteous and holy love. God's love, by definition, adheres to what is good and abhors what is evil. Many people want the kind of God who loves men in their sin, who accepts them "just as they are." God cannot and does not do so, because His love is a righteous love. *But in His love, God has provided a way for us to become holy and righteous, so that His love can be shed abroad in our hearts and lives. The provision is the person of Jesus Christ.* He died in the sinner's place, bearing the penalty for our sins. He offers to us that righteousness which we can never achieve in and of ourselves. *If you would receive the love of God, receive His righteousness, in Christ.*

What the church needs today is "love, sweet love." There is more talk about love than there is the practice of love. And much of that which passes for love is hypocritical. In the name of love, sin is tolerated in the church, rather than rebuked and removed (see, for example, 1 Corinthians 5:1-5). Sometimes sin is practiced in the name of love. This is especially evident in the rampant immorality which is taking place in the church and among Christians.

The love which God calls for is a holy love, a love which hates sin and loves righteousness. The love God calls for is a sacrificial love. It requires us to subordinate our desires and interests, so that we may serve others selflessly. The love which God calls for is one which looks for long-term rewards rather than short-term pleasure. *It endures hardship, suffering, and pain, for the benefit of others and for the service of the King and His pleasure. It is a love which takes risks and which shines forth when others are shrinking back. It is a love which responds to and reflects the love of God for us.*

On another note, it is *a love which gives priority and preference to fellow-Christians—it is a brotherly love.* One of my concerns is that we do not see the church (the body of Christ) or our brethren broadly enough. We desperately need more evidences and expressions of love within our own local church. We need to do better at sharing with those in need and showing hospitality. But the body of Christ is bigger than this. The body of Christ is national and international. When have we shared with a needy group of believers of another race or in another place far, far away? The churches in the Book of Acts did this (see Acts 11:27-30; 2 Corinthians 8-9). The church is not only to show hospitality to those whom we know, but to strangers, whom we do not know, believers who have traveled from faraway places (see Hebrews 13:1-2).

There is a love for the brethren in our church, but it needs to grow. It needs to grow in quantity and in fervency. It also needs to grow outward, to extend to the broader body of Christ. We are instructed not only to demonstrate this love personally but to challenge and stimulate others to "love and good deeds" (Hebrews 10:23-25). May God grant us the grace to do so for His glory.

God's grace and His Mercy.

God, in all His mercy and kindness, has brought a wonderful, God fearing, loving, supportive man into my life who is willing to learn and DO what it takes to have a healthy, loving relationship. Listen beloved if you do not take care of your spouse and family and love them the way God wants you to and if you do not put to use the information that God has given you, God may give them to someone who will. He will not allow you to destroy your spouse and family to the point that they would rather die spiritually than spend another day suffering the pain you inflict on them. Divorce and judgment are never God's perfect will. Repentance and reconciliation are God's perfect will. When someone refuses to repent and reconcile, then judgment takes place and this is God's permissive will. The word "judgment" means "crisis" or "the point where it is decided when something will live or die". It means to be "cut off". God has written and given the instruction manual to us on how to treat and take care of our spouse and children. If we will not follow instructions or do things by God's book or according to God's way, your marriages and the love between you will die. God is attempting to *"Turn the heart of the fathers to the children and the heart of the children to their fathers, lest I come and smite the earth with a curse"*. There is a blessing that comes to those who hear, obey and apply the truth. "But unto you that fear (holy reverence that causes you to listen and apply) my name shall the Sun of righteousness arise with healing in His wings; and ye shall go forth, and grow up as calves of the stall". I have experienced God's mercy, healing, tenderness, compassion and blessing through this person that chooses to follow the "instruction manual" and love me the way God intended. I am blissfully happy and thriving in a healthy, Christian, relationship with someone who is a doer of the word, not just a hearer only. The foundation is on the Rock only when one is a doer of the word. You are not founded on the Rock if you are a hearer only. You must apply the Truth the God gives you to survive the storms that beat against you. Without applying them, your house will fall, because it is founded on the shifting sand. I don't let a day pass without profusely thanking the Lord for the gift He has given me in the man he has brought into my life. I have never felt so much gratitude for anything, ever, other than for my salvation, as I have for this person in my life and the healing he has brought me. God uses him to validate my past hurt and heal them. One such example was when we went grocery shopping together and we needed to buy soap. I asked him what soap he preferred and he said, "Whatever soap you use sweetie will be fine with me". You have no idea the healing impact that his words brought me. God knew. God will supply that which is needed. He is merciful and gracious.

I heard on the radio today that the opposite of love is not hate. The opposite of love is indifference. Indifference to other people's pain and suffering, needs, wants, feelings, etc. That is what I have grown up with. That is what I have been married to in the past. That is what I have encountered in the church. The bible says of Jesus, *"A bruised reed shall he not break and the smoking flax shall he not quench"*. The Jesus I know does not kick you when you are down. He does not break you when you are already so crushed and broken and full of pain that you can take no more. He does not extinguish the flame in you when your spirit or flame is barely lit and the liquid wax is creeping up your wick barely allowing any wick left exposed to burn as it smokes and threatens to extinguish. Jesus doesn't treat these people that way. He offers them a "strong arm". The bible says that God's arm is not too short that it cannot save you and it is never too weak to rescue or deliver you.

How to protect your health against toxic people:

First, think carefully about your own behavior to see if you may have done or said something to cause the other party's behavior.

If you can identify something that you did that likely offended the other party, if possible, offer a sincere apology. If he or she accepts your apology, things work out well for both parties. If your apology is not accepted, you can at least walk away with some peace of mind, knowing that you owned up to your behavior.

If you cannot think of a single thing that you did that could have offended the other party, give him or her a silent "H&G" (Hi and Goodbye) and walk away. Confronting the other party about unkind behavior is not likely to be fruitful. Since you don't have to co-exist on a regular basis, you can take the mindset of "fool me once, shame on you, and fool me twice, shame on me." In other words, the other party's unkind behavior is on him or her; he or she will reap natural consequences in due time. As before, start by examining your own behavior to see if you can come up with a reasonable cause for the other party's unacceptable behavior. If you cannot come up with a reason for the other party's behavior, find someone who you can trust to be as objective and honest as possible, and explain the conflict to him or her as thoroughly and accurately as possible. Ask for honest feedback on how you might have triggered the other party's behavior.

If appropriate, apologize for your behavior. If you and your adviser have thought long and hard about the conflict and cannot identify anything that you need to apologize for, work on developing compassion for the other party.

Most will agree that people are not born to be mean-spirited and toxic to others. People can *become* mean-spirited and toxic to others for varying periods of time if they encounter enough hurt, disappointment, and/or anger in their own journeys. Maybe the other party is jealous of you and consumed by his or her own failures. Maybe he or she is just going through a really rough time due to a loss in the family. Maybe he or she has never truly felt cared about by another person. Maybe the other party has been treated so poorly by family members that sensitivity has been numbed and he or she has no idea that you feel like you have been mistreated. The idea is to generate enough compassion for the other person to overpower or at least quell your hurt feelings.

This doesn't mean that you need to be a martyr or a doormat and go asking for another three tight slaps to your other cheek. Developing some compassion for the other party's behavior is meant to prevent said behavior from causing you to stew and stay emotionally unbalanced for a long time after the actual moment of conflict. And if the other party has or develops the courage to apologize to you, having some pre-made compassion available in your heart improves your chances of offering genuine forgiveness and experiencing that much more emotional harmony.

After you have worked on developing compassion for the other person's circumstances, if you haven't received an apology, be kind, but don't push for a make-up session. An important part of experiencing emotional balance is learning to teach others that you expect to be treated with kindness and respect. To seek out a make-up session when you have done nothing wrong and the other party has not mustered up the courage to apologize is to teach him or her that you can be walked on - not a good lesson to give.

~I Will Never Leave You nor Forsake You~

There are four stages that an abused person goes through. The last stage is the stage of abandonment. This is where you feel abandoned by God and others who claim to be followers of

God. The victim of abuse says thing like, "Why are you letting this happen, God? Why don't you do something? If you were just here, this wouldn't have happened". God understands and validates these feelings of abandonment and He weeps when we feel abandoned by Him. This is what He has shown me. When Lazarus died, one of his sisters said to Jesus, "Lord, if you had just been here, this wouldn't have happened". The shortest verse in the bible follows and it reads, "Jesus wept". Jesus didn't weep because Lazarus died. He knew Lazarus would be raised from the dead and God would be glorified. Jesus wept because Lazarus' sister felt abandoned by God. Jesus weeps when we suffer and when we feel abandoned by God. Some of my favorite versus in the bible are, "I will never leave you or forsake you. I will not leave you comfortless. I will send you a comforter". The Lord addresses and validates the abandonment issue of victims of abuse. He has always validated my feelings and has shown me that He is here, knows of my feelings and situation and He weeps when we feel abandoned by Him.

The name "Joanne" is a Hebrew name meaning: Divine oracle or God is gracious. Literally translated it means that God will supply you with whatever it is you need. God has used my name many times in ministering to me and confirming, not only the call that is on my life, but in instilling faith in me in my hour of greatest need. God has truly been gracious and faithful to supply me with whatever it is I needed, including this new man in my life after judgment/crisis/or the cutting off of the marriage was determined. God had tried to dig around the tree that was bringing forth no fruit. He had fertilized it and watered it with the truth and He had checked it and supplied it with more and been long suffering with the abuser in producing fruit, only to find that none had grown. The

Lord has said, "Cut it down. Don't let it burden the earth anymore". So be it. Just as the marriage ceremony is an external ritual that shows what has already transpired in the hearts of two lovers, so is divorce. Divorce is just the ritual or legality of something that has already transpired in the hearts of two people. Marriage doesn't make you fall in love. Marriage is the result of two people falling in love and divorce is the result of two people not being able to love because of selfishness and pain. A piece of paper or a ring does not make one married and vice versa regarding divorce. It is just the outcome or result of something that has already transpired in the heart and God looks at the heart. My marriage to the abuser was long since dead, irreconcilable and not able to be saved long before divorce proceedings ever were started because of the denial the abuser was in and his inability to repent or "change his mind". Repentance is necessary for reconciliation and it is a requirement that God has of us in order that we be reconciled to Him and it is, also, necessary in our relationships. Please remember this the next time you deny, justify, rationalize, explain, give your intent and minimize your behavior in order that you do not have to "repent or change your mind". A man who covers his sin with the above techniques will not prosper. It doesn't work. You are throwing gasoline on the fire, not water. You are accomplishing the opposite of what you are trying to accomplish. There is a way that seems right unto a man that leads to destruction, as the bible states, and this is it. God's way works! Man's way does not. I have set before you this day, blessing or cursing, life or death. Choose you this day whom you will serve.

CHAPTER FOUR

~Detach-Let Them Go!~

Detaching from a toxic person can take some time and much, much prayer! Either they can pull you in or you can break free the choice is up you! [8]Erykah Badu's song "Bag Lady" is a prime example of the healing power of music, and the lessons that can be taught through music. Erykah Badu's "Bag Lady" serves as a <u>wakeup call</u> for women and men across the world. From the first verse of the song until the last verse when the song begins to fade, Badu's words evoke feelings of emotion that women can relate to. Badu's lyrics also help women find some type of inner peace to get over their problems, in a way that will best help them free their spirit. Although I do not follow her music or her religion I do understand why she wrote that song and can attest the feelings behind it all.

What is detachment? Detachment is the: Ability to allow people, places or things the freedom to be themselves. Holding back from the need to rescue, save or fix another person from being sick, dysfunctional or irrational. Giving another person "the space" to be herself. Disengaging from an over-enmeshed or dependent relationship with people. Willingness to accept that you cannot change or control a person, place or thing. Developing and maintaining of a safe, emotional distance from someone whom you have previously given a lot of power to affect your emotional

Establishing of emotional boundaries between you and those people you have become overly enmeshed or dependent with in order that all of you might be able to develop your own sense of autonomy and independence. *Process by which you are free to feel your own feelings when you see another person falter and fail and not be led by guilt to feel responsible for their failure or faltering. *Ability to maintain an emotional bond of love, concern and caring without the negative results of rescuing, enabling, fixing or controlling. *Placing of all things in life into a healthy, rational perspective and recognizing that there is a need to back away from the uncontrollable and unchangeable realities of lift *Ability to exercise emotional self-protection and prevention so as not to experience greater emotional devastation from having hung on beyond a reasonable and rational point. *Ability to let people you love and care for accept personal responsibility for their own actions and to practice tough love and not give in when they come to you to bail them out when their actions lead to failure or trouble for them. * Ability to allow people to be who they "really are" rather than who you "want them to be." * Ability to avoid being hurt, abused, taken advantage of by people who in the past have been overly dependent or enmeshed with you.

What are the negative effects not detaching? If you are unable to detach from people, places or things, then you: * Will have people, places or things which become over-dependent on you. * Run the risk of being manipulated to do things for people, at places or with things which you do not really want to do. * Can become an obsessive "fix it" who needs to fix everything you perceive to be imperfect. * Run the risk of performing tasks because of the intimidation you experience from people, places or things. * Will most probably become powerless in the face of the demands of the people, places or things whom you have given the power to control you. * Will be blind to the reality that the people, places or things which control you are the uncontrollables and unchangeables you need to let go of if you are to become a fully healthy, coping individual. * Will be easily influenced by the perception of helplessness which these people, places or things project. * Might become caught up with your idealistic need to make everything perfect for people, places or things important to you even if it means your own life becomes unhealthy. * Run the risk of becoming out of control of yourself and experience greater low self-esteem as a result. * Will most probably put off making a decision and following through on it, if you rationally recognize your relationship with a person, place or thing is unhealthy and the only recourse left is to get out of the relationship. * Will be so driven by guilt and emotional dependence that the sickness in the relationship will worsen. * Run the risk of losing your autonomy and independence and derive your value or worth solely from the unhealthy relationship you continue in with the unhealthy person, place or thing.

How is detachment a control issue? Detachment is a control issue because: * It is a way of de-powering the external "locus of control" issues in your life and a way to strengthen your internal "locus of control." * If you are not able to detach emotionally or physically from a person, place or thing, then you are either profoundly under its control or it is under your control. * The ability to "keep distance" emotionally or physically requires self-control and the inability to do so is a sign that you are "out of control." * If you are not able to detach from another person, place or thing, you might be powerless over this behavior which is beyond your personal control. * You might be mesmerized, brainwashed or psychically in a trance when you are in the presence of someone from whom you cannot detach. * You might feel intimidated or coerced to stay deeply attached with someone for fear of great harm to yourself or that person if you don't remain so deeply involved. * You might be an addicted caretaker, fixer or rescuer who cannot let go of a person, place or thing you believe cannot care for itself. * You might be so manipulated by another's con, "helplessness," overdependence or "hooks" that you cannot leave them to solve their own problems. * If you do not detach from people, places or things, you could be so busy trying to "control" them that you completely divert your attention from yourself and your own needs. * By being "selfless" and "centered" on other people, you are really a controller trying to fix them to meet the image of your ideal for them. * Although you will still have feelings for those persons, places and things from which you have become detached, you will have given them the freedom to become what they will be on their own merit, power, control and responsibility. * It allows every person, place or thing with which you become involved to feel the sense of personal responsibility to become a unique, independent and autonomous being with no fear of retribution or rebuke if they don't please you by what they become.

How to Develop Detachment In order to become detached from a person, place or thing, you need to:

First: Establish emotional boundaries between you and the person, place or thing with whom you have become overly enmeshed or dependent on.

Second: Take back power over your feelings from persons, places or things which in the past you have given power to affect your emotional well-being.

Third: "Hand over" to your Heavenly Father the persons, places and things which you would like to see changed but which you cannot change on your own.

Fourth: Make a commitment to your personal recovery and self-health by admitting to yourself and your Heavenly Father that there is only one person you can change and that is yourself and that for your serenity you need to let go of the "need" to fix, change, rescue or heal other persons, places and things.

Fifth: Recognize that it is "sick" and "unhealthy" to believe that you have the power or control enough to fix, correct, change, heal or rescue another person, place or thing if they do not want to get better nor see a need to change.

Sixth: Recognize that you need to be healthy yourself and be "squeaky clean" and a "role model" of health in order for another to recognize that there is something "wrong" with them that needs changing.

Seventh: Continue to own your feelings as your responsibility and not blame others for the way you feel.

Eighth: Accept personal responsibility for your own unhealthy actions, feelings and thinking and cease looking for the persons, places or things you can blame for your unhealthiness.

Ninth: Accept that addicted fixing, rescuing, enabling are "sick" behaviors and strive to extinguish these behaviors in your relationship to persons, places and things.

Tenth: Accept that many people, places and things in your past and current life are "irrational," "unhealthy" and "toxic" influences in your life, label them honestly for what they truly are, and stop minimizing their negative impact in your life.

Eleventh: Reduce the impact of guilt and other irrational beliefs which impede your ability to develop detachment in your life.

Twelfth: Practice "letting go" of the need to correct, fix or make better the persons, places and things in life over which you have no control or power to change.

Steps in Developing Detachment

Step 1: It is important to first identify those people, places and things in your life from which you would be best to develop emotional detachment in order to retain your personal, physical, emotional and spiritual health. To do this you need to review the following types of toxic relationships and identify in your journal if any of the people, places or things in your life fit any of the following 20 categories.

Step 2: Once you have identified the persons, places and things you have a toxic relationship with, then you need to take each one individually and work through the following **steps.**

Step 3: Identify the irrational beliefs in the toxic relationship which prevent you from becoming detached. Address these beliefs and replace them with healthy, more rational ones.

Step 4: Identify all of the reasons why you are being hurt and your physical, emotional and spiritual health is being threatened by the relationship.

Step 5: Accept and admit to yourself that the other person, place or thing is "sick," dysfunctional or irrational, and that no matter what you say, do or demand you will not be able to control or change this reality. Accept that there is only one thing you can change in life and that is you. All others are the unchangeable in your life. Change your expectations that things will be better than what they really are. Hand these people, places or things over to your Higher Power and let go of the need to change them.

Step 6: Work out reasons why there is no need to feel guilt over letting go and being emotionally detached from this relationship and free yourself from guilt as you let go of the emotional "hooks" in the relationship.

Step 7: Affirm yourself as being a person who "deserves" healthy, wholesome, health-engendering relationships in your life. You are a good person and deserve healthy relationships, at home, work and in the community.

Step 8: Gain support for yourself as you begin to let go of your emotional enmeshment with these relationships.

Step 9: Continue to call upon your Higher Power for the strength to continue to let go and detach

Step 10: Continue to give no person, place or thing the power to affect or impact your feelings about yourself.

Step 11: Continue to detach and let go and work at self-recovery and self-healing as this poem implies.

"Letting Go"

* To "let go" does not mean to stop caring; it means I can't do it for someone else.

 * To "let go" is not to cut myself off; it's the realization I can't control another.

 * To "let go" is not to enable, but to allow learning from natural consequences.

 * To "let go" is to admit powerlessness, which means the outcome is not in my hands.

 * To "let go" is not to try to change or blame another; it's to make the most of myself.

* To "let go" is not to care for, but to care about.

* To "let go" is not to fix, but to be supportive.

* To "let go" is not to judge, but to allow another to be a human being.

* To "let go" is not to be in the middle arranging all the outcomes, but to allow others to affect their own destinies.

* To "let go" is not to be protective; it's to permit another to face reality.

* To "let go" is not to deny, but to accept.

* To "let go" is not to nag, scold or argue, but instead to search out my own shortcomings and correct them.

* To "let go" is not to criticize and regulate anybody, but to try to become what I dream I can be.

* To "let go" is not to adjust everything to my desires, but to take each day as it comes and cherish myself in it.

* To "let go" is to not regret the past, but to grow and live for the future.

* To "let go" is to fear less and love myself more.

Step 12: If you still have problems detaching, then return to Step 1 and begin all over again.

Now Bishop T.D. Jakes couple years ago came up with this lovely poem and I believe wholeheartedly everyone should have this in their home hanging in a frame and its called [7]Let it go! If you don't have it already go get yourself a copy…read those words and see for yourself! Your life will change dramatically when you speak positively.

CHAPTER FIVE

~You Are A Winner!~

Greater is HE that is in you than he that is in the world! Do you know that you are a winner on the inside of you! No longer should you allow anyone to pull you down to their negative energy or their toxicity! You can defeat the enemy and that negative energy by speaking life in your situation IMMEDIATELY! Catch it before it escalates and seeps in your inner being (spirit man)!

Now there is a humorous side how you can handle a toxic person and your response can, for example, defuse the toxic person, so try laughing at your "snide" friends instead of getting angry. Alternatively, mirroring their behavior can show them how unreasonable they're being, while other situations call for a calmer, more questioning approach. Sometimes, if the person is particularly obnoxious, the only way to deal with them is to lose your temper.

But just deciding to do something about the toxic people in your life is a big step in itself. You might know you should detox from your friend/partner/boss, but it's not always that easy to do it. Okay you can find other friends, partners and jobs, but you can't, for instance, go out and choose a new mother.

I couldn't understand why God would want me to write something like this so personal. So hurtful where it opened up some old wounds but God told me, *how I can heal you fully and your family and your generation if you don't allow me to expose what's going on the inside of your hearts?!!* For my God doesn't operate in confusion!! *"For God is not the author of confusion but of peace, as in all the churches of the saints." 1 Corinthians 14:33 NKJV* So I submitted to what God wanted me to do! So please don't be upset because I tell the truth *("but speaking the truth in love, may grow up in all things into Him who is the Head-Christ" Ephesians 4:15 NKJV)* or expose what the devil wanted to keep hidden! The devil is liar!! *("You are of your father the devil, and the desires of your father you want to do. He was a murderer from the beginning, and does not stand in the truth, because there is no truth in him. When he speaks a lie, he speaks from his own resources, for he is a liar and the father of it." John 8:44 NKJV)*

Here are some scriptures that you can meditate upon as well:

Psalm 16:6 *"The boundary lines have fallen for me in pleasant places; surely I have a delightful inheritance."*

Matthew 5:43–48, *"You have heard that it was said, 'Love your neighbor and hate your enemy.' But I tell you: Love your enemies and pray for those who persecute you, that you may be sons of your Father in heaven. He causes his sun to rise on the evil and the good, and sends rain on the righteous and the unrighteous. If you love those who love you, what reward will you get? Are not even the tax collectors doing that? And if you greet only your brothers, what are you doing more than others? Do not even pagans do that? Be perfect, therefore, as your heavenly Father is perfect."*

Romans 12:18NLT, *"Do all that you can to live in peace with everyone."*

Galatians 6:9NIV, *"Let us not become weary in doing good, for at the proper time we will reap a harvest if we do not give up."*

Philippians 4:8, NIV" *Finally, brothers, whatever is true, whatever is noble, whatever is right, whatever is pure, whatever is lovely, whatever is admirable--if anything is excellent or praiseworthy--think about such things."*

~Conclusion~

Generally speaking, I think it's safe to say that a person is toxic to your health if his or her behavior makes you feel bad on a regular basis. Clearly, there are exceptions to this guideline. For example, if a close friend or family member shares a concern about your behavior with a spirit of wanting to improve your relationship, you may feel bad and your sense of emotional well-being may take a temporary hit, but it doesn't make sense to label such friends or family members as being toxic.

What follows are specific patterns of behavior that I believe fall into the "toxic-to-your-health" category:
- A. Attempting to intimidate you by yelling or becoming violent in any manner (slamming a door **is** a violent act).
- B. Consistently talking down at you, sending the message that he or she is just plain better than you.
- C. Regularly telling you what he or she thinks is wrong with you.
- D. Slandering others behind their backs i.e. trying to engage you in gossip that is hurtful to others.
- E. Spending the bulk of your conversations complaining about his or her life and others.
- F. Discouraging you from pursuing your interests and dreams.
- G. Attempting to take advantage of your kindness and resources, and trying to make you feel guilty if you don't do what he or she wants.

More Signs for Toxic People in Your Life

Here are more signs below for "Toxic People" in your life when it comes with your loved ones. Please take note of the signs and take it seriously. Don't put it off because it may be detrimental to you or even life threatening! God loves you and he doesn't want you to be harmed or you harm someone else. Seek help fast! Don't put it off as to think that person will change or better yet thinking you can change them. Seek spiritual guidance and most of all PRAYER IS THE KEY! Pray for that individual immediately! If none of those things work -- GET OUT!!!

1) Your spouse puts you down verbally, in private or in front of others.
2) Your spouse tells you he/she loves you but behavior shows otherwise.
3) Your spouse doesn't want you to see or talk to friends or family.
4) Your spouse is jealous of the time you spend with your kids.
5) Your spouse shows up often at your work unexpectedly or opens your mail.
6) Your spouse calls you often to see what you are doing.
7) You cry often or feel depressed over your relationship.
8) Your spouse says you would have the perfect relationship if only you would change.
9) Your spouse wants you to be dependent on him.
10) Your spouse does things for you and then uses them to make you feel obligated.

11) Your thoughts, opinions, accomplishments, or words are devalued.
12) You don't know who you are anymore without him/her, or how you would survive.
13) Your friends/family doesn't like your spouse/partner or don't think he/she is good for you but never tell you the reason always negative towards them when they come around.
14) You have changed things about yourself to suit your spouse/partner, even when it is not your taste.
15) You always go where your spouse/partner wants to, like movies, restaurants, etc never given the options of your likes/dislikes.
16) Your spouse/partner has made you feel afraid or unsafe, and you have been afraid to speak the truth at times for fear of upsetting him/her (walking on eggshells).
17) You don't feel you have control of your life anymore.
18) Your self-esteem is lower since you've been with your spouse/partner.
20) You keep secrets about your relationship from others who love you because they wouldn't understand.
21) Your spouse/partner makes you feel unattractive or stupid.
22) Your spouse/partner accuses you of cheating and is overly jealous.
23) Your spouse/partner can be really sweet to you one minute, and really mean the next.
24) Your spouse/partner seems really sweet/loving to you when he/she thinks you are about to leave the relationship, or after he/she has been mean to you.

25) You can't remember the last time you felt happy for more than a few days straight.

⁵Being able to experience Godly relationships is a gift from God. As we share our needs with another person, the result is mutual contribution of similar interests, ideals, and experiences that develop into personal interaction. For Godly relationships to develop and flourish we must not reject the truth about ourselves, going regularly to the cross, where the ground is always level and we are met with open arms.

To better understand the relationships God would have you develop, commit to undertake this prayer series for 31 days by taking the following steps:

READ the assigned Scripture passage silently first; then out loud.
MEDITATE on what you have read.
PRAY the passage back to God. Ask for wisdom and understanding.
APPLY what you have learned to your life each day.

DAY1: Psalm 133

DAY2: Proverbs 17:17

DAY3: Romans 12:10

DAY4: 1 Thessalonians 4:9-10

DAY5: John 13:34-35

DAY6: Romans 13:8

DAY7: Ephesians 4:2

DAY8 : 1 Peter 1:22

DAY9: 1 Peter 3:8

DAY10: 1 John 4:7

DAY 11: 1 Corinthians 13

DAY 12: John 3:16

DAY 13: Romans 12:16

DAY 14: Proverbs 27:9

DAY 15: 1 Samuel 20:41-42

DAY 16: Ecclesiastes 4:9-11

DAY 17: John 15:12-15

DAY 18: James 2:23

DAY 19: Isaiah 9:6

DAY 20: John 14:26

DAY 21: John 15:26

DAY 22: John 16:7

DAY 23: Ruth 1:16-17

DAY 24: Acts 2:42-47

DAY 25: Matthew 5:25

DAY 26: Romans 14:10

DAY 27: Romans 6:1-11

DAY 28: James 4:11

DAY 29: Matthew 18:19-21

DAY 30: Ephesians 4:16

DAY 31: Ephesians 3:17-19

If you need help with your relationship, talk to a friend or family member, a clergyman, a counselor, or call your local mental health center. If you are in danger, help is available at [4]The National Domestic Violence Hotline, (800) 799-SAFE, where someone can put you in touch with battered women's shelters and other resources. Remember, no one can take care of you as well as YOU can. Get the help you need.

I pray that this book will bring healing, hope and a closer relationship to Jesus as it reveals what the Lord really feels about abuse and divorce. Let the Truth set you free from all the judgmental and legalistic, shaming attitudes in the church or in families. Please know that God has directed you here and He wants you to be set free with the Truth. Whatever it is that you need, Jesus will supply it for you. Need hope, strength, the ability to forgive, finances, love, mercy, validation, kindness or anything else, go to Jesus. He is the source of that and that is what is meant by Jesus being the Life. Ask Him into your heart, read the bible, talk to Him and have a relationship with Him. He is waiting for you with open arms full of love and mercy. Be blessed!

~Prayer~

Father, help me to develop godly relationships in my life. Give me discernment concerning the friendships I make.

Lord, I realize the wrong friendships can be a destructive force in my life. Help me to let go of any relationship that pulls me away from you and Your Word. Help me to recognize any relationship in my life that is codependent, and give me insight to correct or end that relationship.

Lead me to friends who love you and have a close relationship with you. Help me to be sensitive to the needs of my friends, and to encourage them in their spiritual walk. May You, Lord, be at the center of all my friendships.

Lord, help me to develop honest, trustworthy, and loyal friendships. Help us to speak truth about areas in each other's life that need improvement. Help us to not be offended but thankful that we love each other enough to speak the truth.

Give me your wisdom, Lord, to build healthy relationships that will last a lifetime. In Jesus Name AMEN!

Endnotes:

1. Norman Hillyer, *New International Biblical Commentary: 1 and 2 Peter, Jude,* Peabody, MA: Hendrickson Publishers, 1992, p. 258.
2. Ibid., p. 258, quoting Barcley, W., *The Letters of James and Peter,* Revised ed., Philadelphia: Westminster, 1975 p. 198.
3. Quoting *Commentary on Jude,* Gerald Bray, Ed., *Ancient Christian Commentary on Scripture: James, 1-2 Peter, 1-3 John, Jude,* Downers Grove, IL: Intervarsity Press, 2000, p. 255.
4. The National Domestic Violence Hotline., www.thehotline.org
5. Pray for Godly Relationships by Althea DeBrule, Christian Career Tools 2011.
6. Changes That Heal, by Dr. Henry Cloud
7. Let it Go, by Bishop TD Jakes
8. Virtue, song "My Body"
9. Erykah Badu song "Bag Lady"
10. R. Kelly, song "When a Woman's Fed up!"
11. Joseph Fletcher philosopher recognized for "Moral theory and applied Christian ethics."
12. NKJV, You-Version online bible-1982 by Thomas Nelson, Inc. (www.youversion.com)
13. NLT (NEW LIVING TRANSLATION)-TYNDALE Life Application Study Bible 1988
14. NIV (NEW INTERNATIONAL VERSION)-ZONDERVAN Holy Bible 1984